Taste of Home Make Ahead FAVORITES

TASTE OF HOME BOOKS • RDA ENTHUSIAST BRANDS, LLC • MILWAUKEE, WI

© 2022 RDA Enthusiast Brands, LLC.
1610 N. 2nd St., Suite 102,
Milwaukee, WI 53212-3906
All rights reserved. Taste of Home is a registered
trademark of RDA Enthusiast Brands, LLC.

Visit us at tasteofhome.com for other
Taste of Home books and products.

International Standard Book Number:
978-1-62145-791-6

Component Number:
116700111H

Executive Editor: Mark Hagen
Senior Art Director: Raeann Thompson
Senior Editor: Christine Rukavena
Editor: Hazel Wheaton
Senior Designer: Jazmin Delgado
Deputy Editor, Copy Desk: Dulcie Shoener
Copy Editor: Elizabeth Pollock Bruch
Contributing Designer: Jennifer Ruetz

Photographer: Jim Wieland
Set Stylist: Stacey Genaw
Food Stylist: Shannon Norris

Pictured on front cover:
Pizza Noodle Bake, p. 41
Pictured on title page:
Balsamic Beef Hoagies, p. 40
Pictured on back cover:
Coffee-Braised Roast Beef, p. 40;
Fried Ice Cream Dessert Bars, p. 106;
Fire-Roasted Tomato Minestrone, p. 34

Printed in USA
1 3 5 7 9 10 8 6 4 2

P. 68

P. 46

P. 25

P. 58

Dig into bubbling casseroles, cheesy pizzas, satisfying soups and stews, and desserts layered with flavor. It's easy to enjoy these classics no matter how hectic your schedule is! All you need is bit of forethought and the right recipes—and that's where **Make Ahead Favorites** comes into play.

Inside you'll find 137 dishes offering all the fix-it-and-forget-it convenience that busy cooks crave. From freezer-friendly entrees that reheat in a jiffy to slow-cooked dinners ready when you are, the recipes in this all-new cookbook beat the clock every time.

You'll even discover buttery biscuits, holiday sides, egg bakes, marinated meats, pasta salads, pastries and other overnight specialties that set up on their own in the fridge. What could be easier?

You'll also enjoy...

• A freezer icon ❄ spotlighting dishes that freeze well. You'll find reheating directions with these recipes, too!

• A slow-cooker icon 🍲 that makes it a snap to find the classics that simmer to perfection on their own.

• Fantastic breakfast and brunch delights that sit in the fridge ready to bake in the morning.

• Appetizers you can assemble days in advance, saving time (and stress) on the day of your party.

• Sweet snacks and desserts to store in the freezer for last-minute treats.

Whether you need new staples to round out your meal planner or you're simply looking to load up the freezer with go-to greats, **Make Ahead Favorites** helps you set the table for succulent success!

More ways to connect with us: 

SHOPTASTEOFHOME.COM

CONTENTS

P. 79

P. 109

BUFFALO CHICKEN
SLIDERS, P. 13

Snacks & Appetizers

Make your next party as effortless as can be by preparing your appetizers in advance, avoiding a last-minute rush on the big day!

MAKE-AHEAD
SAUSAGE PINWHEELS, P. 12

MINI PHYLLO TACOS

These quick appetizers are irresistible on the plate, and the flavors of sun-dried tomatoes and pesto balance beautifully!
—*Kristen Heigl, Staten Island, NY*

PREP: 20 min. + freezing • **BAKE:** 15 min.
MAKES: 16 appetizers

- 1 sheet frozen puff pastry, thawed
- 1 pkg. (8 oz.) cream cheese, softened
- ¼ cup prepared pesto
- ¾ cup shredded provolone cheese
- ½ cup chopped oil-packed sun-dried tomatoes
- ½ cup chopped ripe olives
- ¼ tsp. pepper

1. Unfold puff pastry; roll out and trim into a 10-in. square.
2. Beat cream cheese and pesto until smooth; stir in the remaining ingredients. Spread cheese mixture on pastry to within ½ in. of edges. Roll up jelly-roll style. Freeze for 30 minutes.
3. Preheat oven to 400°. Cut roll crosswise into 16 slices. Bake slices cut side down on a parchment-lined baking sheet until golden brown, 12-15 minutes.

Freeze option: Cover and freeze unbaked pastry slices on waxed paper-lined baking sheets until firm. Transfer slices to airtight container; return to freezer. To use, bake in a preheated 400° oven until golden brown, 15-20 minutes.

1 appetizer: 170 cal., 13g fat (5g sat. fat), 18mg chol., 227mg sod., 11g carb. (1g sugars, 2g fiber), 4g pro.

TEST KITCHEN TIP
Once it is opened, wrap unused puff pastry tightly; it will keep in the refrigerator for up to 3 days or in the freezer for up to a month.

❄
MINI PHYLLO TACOS

Crispy phyllo cups are the secret to creating an appetizer with all the flavor and appeal of a taco—without the mess! The two-bite treats of spicy ground beef and zesty shredded cheese will be a surefire hit with a hungry crowd.
—*Roseann Weston, Philipsburg, PA*

PREP: 30 min. • **BAKE:** 10 min.
MAKES: 2½ dozen

- 1 lb. lean ground beef (90% lean)
- ½ cup finely chopped onion
- 1 envelope taco seasoning
- ¾ cup water
- 1¼ cups shredded Mexican cheese blend, divided
- 2 pkg. (1.9 oz. each) frozen miniature phyllo tart shells

1. Preheat oven to 350°. In a small skillet, cook beef and onion over medium heat until the meat is no longer pink, breaking into crumbles; drain. Stir in taco seasoning and water. Bring to a boil. Reduce heat; simmer, uncovered, about 5 minutes. Remove from heat; stir in ½ cup cheese blend.
2. Place tart shells in an ungreased 15x10x1-in. baking pan. Fill with taco mixture.
3. Bake for 6 minutes. Sprinkle with remaining ¾ cup cheese blend; bake until the cheese is melted, 2-3 minutes longer.

Freeze option: Freeze cooled taco cups in a freezer container, separating layers with waxed paper. To use, reheat on a baking sheet in a preheated 350° oven until crisp and heated through.

1 appetizer: 63 cal., 3g fat (1g sat. fat), 11mg chol., 156mg sod., 4g carb. (0 sugars, 0 fiber), 4g pro.

MEDITERRANEAN
PASTRY PINWHEELS

CHEESE CRISPIES

For years I've taken these crispy, crunchy snacks to work. They always get high marks from everybody in the teachers lounge.
—*Eileen Ball, Cornelius, NC*

PREP: 15 min. + chilling • **BAKE:** 15 min./batch
MAKES: about 4½ dozen

1	cup unsalted butter, softened
2½	cups shredded extra-sharp cheddar cheese
2	cups all-purpose flour
¾	tsp. salt
½	tsp. cayenne pepper
2½	cups Rice Krispies
	Pecan halves, optional

1. Beat butter and cheese until blended. In another bowl, whisk flour, salt and cayenne; gradually beat into the cheese mixture. Stir in Rice Krispies. If necessary, turn onto a lightly floured surface and knead 4-6 times, forming a stiff dough.

2. Divide dough in half; shape each half into a 7-in.-long roll. Wrap and refrigerate for 1 hour or overnight.

3. Preheat oven to 350°. Unwrap dough and cut rolls crosswise into ¼-in. slices. Place 1 in. apart on parchment-lined baking sheets. If desired, top each slice with a pecan half. Bake until edges are golden brown, 14-16 minutes. Remove from pans to wire racks to cool.

To make ahead: Dough can be made 2 days in advance.

Freeze option: Freeze wrapped logs in an airtight container. To use, unwrap frozen logs and cut into slices. Bake as directed.

1 cracker: 73 cal., 5g fat (3g sat. fat), 15mg chol., 73mg sod., 5g carb. (0 sugars, 0 fiber), 2g pro.

MAKE-AHEAD EGGNOG

Sipping homemade eggnog is a holiday tradition for many families. Our slow-cooker version of the classic drink couldn't be easier to make.
—Taste of Home *Test Kitchen*

PREP: 10 min. • **COOK:** 2 hours
MAKES: 9 servings

6	cups whole milk
1	cup egg substitute
⅔	cup sugar
2	tsp. rum extract
1½	tsp. pumpkin pie spice
	French vanilla whipped topping, optional

In a 3-qt. slow cooker, combine the first 5 ingredients. Cover and cook on low until heated through, 2-3 hours. Serve in mugs; dollop with whipped topping if desired.

¾ cup: 174 cal., 5g fat (3g sat. fat), 16mg chol., 121mg sod., 23g carb. (23g sugars, 0 fiber), 8g pro.

TEST KITCHEN TIP
Rather than buying a commercial blend, you can make your own pumpkin pie spice by mixing 4 tsp. cinnamon, 2 tsp. ginger, 1 tsp. cloves and ½ tsp. nutmeg.

CHEESE CRISPIES

MAKE-AHEAD SPINACH
PHYLLO APPETIZERS

SAUSAGE WONTON CUPS

Here's a tasty hot appetizer for all those parties that feature fun finger foods. I've made this recipe several times, and these bites always disappear fast. It's really easy.
—*Shirley Van Allen, High Point, NC*

TAKES: 30 min. • **MAKES:** 2 dozen

- 1 lb. Italian turkey sausage links, casings removed
- 1 can (15 oz.) tomato sauce
- ½ tsp. garlic powder
- ½ tsp. dried basil
- 24 wonton wrappers
- 1 cup shredded Italian cheese blend

1. In a large skillet, cook sausage over medium heat until no longer pink; drain. Stir in the tomato sauce, garlic powder and basil. Bring to a boil. Reduce heat; simmer, uncovered, until thickened, 8-10 minutes.
2. Meanwhile, press wonton wrappers into miniature muffin cups coated with cooking spray. Bake at 350° until lightly browned, 8-9 minutes.
3. Spoon sausage mixture into cups. Sprinkle with cheese. Bake until the cheese is melted, 5-7 minutes longer. Serve warm.
Freeze option: Cool appetizers; freeze them in freezer containers, separating layers with waxed paper. To use, reheat wonton cups in coated muffin pans in a preheated 350° oven until crisp and heated through.

1 wonton cup: 68 cal., 3g fat (1g sat. fat), 15mg chol., 270mg sod., 6g carb. (0 sugars, 0 fiber), 5g pro. **Diabetic exchanges:** ½ starch, ½ fat.

MAKE-AHEAD SPINACH PHYLLO APPETIZERS

I love having appetizers on hand in the freezer, especially when the holiday season is fast approaching. This easy recipe is one of my all-time favorites. Everyone loves them, they're easy to prepare and they bake up in about 20 minutes.
—*Shannon Dobos, Calgary, AB*

PREP: 45 min. • **BAKE:** 15 min.
MAKES: 2½ dozen

- 2 pkg. (10 oz. each) frozen chopped spinach, thawed and squeezed dry
- 1 pkg. (8 oz.) cream cheese, softened
- ½ cup crumbled feta cheese
- 2 large eggs, lightly beaten
- ¼ cup finely chopped onion
- ¼ cup mayonnaise
- 2 Tbsp. snipped fresh dill
- ¾ tsp. seasoned salt
- ¼ tsp. pepper
- 15 sheets phyllo dough (14x9-in. size)
- ½ cup butter, melted
  Optional: Tzatziki sauce, lemon wedges and fresh dill sprigs

1. Preheat oven to 425°. In a large bowl, mix the first 9 ingredients. Place 1 sheet of phyllo dough on a work surface; brush with butter. Layer with 2 additional phyllo sheets, brushing each layer. (Keep remaining phyllo covered with plastic wrap and a damp towel to prevent it from drying out.)
2. Arrange ¾ cup spinach mixture in a narrow row along the long end of phyllo to within 1 in. of edges. Fold bottom edge of phyllo over filling, then roll up. Brush end of phyllo dough with butter and press to seal. Repeat 4 times with phyllo sheets, butter and the spinach mixture. Place rolls on a parchment-lined 15x10x1-in. baking pan, seam side down.
3. Cut rolls diagonally into 2-in. pieces (do not separate). Brush tops with remaining butter. Bake until golden brown, 12-15 minutes. If desired, serve with tzatziki sauce, lemon wedges and dill sprigs.
Freeze option: Cover and freeze unbaked rolls on a parchment-lined baking sheet until firm. Transfer to a freezer container; return to freezer. To use, bake rolls on a parchment-lined 15x10x1-in. baking pan in a preheated 375° oven until heated through and golden brown, about 25 minutes.

1 piece: 96 cal., 8g fat (4g sat. fat), 29mg chol., 155mg sod., 5g carb. (1g sugars, 1g fiber), 2g pro.

BUTTER CHICKEN
MEATBALLS

BUTTER CHICKEN MEATBALLS

My husband and I love meatballs, and we love butter chicken. Before an appetizer party, we had the brilliant idea to combine these two loves, and they got rave reviews! Want them as a main dish? Just serve with basmati rice.
—*Shannon Dobos, Calgary, AB*

PREP: 30 min. • **COOK:** 3 hours
MAKES: about 3 dozen

- 1½ **lbs. ground chicken or turkey**
- 1 **large egg, lightly beaten**
- ½ **cup soft bread crumbs**
- 1 **tsp. garam masala**
- ½ **tsp. tandoori masala seasoning**
- ½ **tsp. salt**
- ¼ **tsp. cayenne pepper**
- 3 **Tbsp. minced fresh cilantro, divided**
- 1 **jar (14.1 oz.) butter chicken sauce**

1. Combine the first 7 ingredients plus 2 Tbsp. cilantro; mix lightly but thoroughly. With wet hands, shape into 1-in. balls. Place meatballs in a 3-qt. slow cooker coated with cooking spray. Pour butter sauce over meatballs.

2. Cook, covered, on low until the meatballs are cooked through, 3-4 hours. Top with the remaining 1 Tbsp. cilantro.

Freeze option: Omitting 1 Tbsp. remaining cilantro, freeze cooled meatball mixture in freezer containers. To use, partially thaw in refrigerator overnight. Microwave, covered, on high in a microwave-safe dish until heated through, stirring gently and adding a little water if necessary. To serve, sprinkle with remaining cilantro.

Note: To make soft bread crumbs, tear bread into pieces and place in a food processor or blender. Cover and pulse until crumbs form. One slice of bread yields ½ to ¾ cup crumbs.

1 meatball: 40 cal., 2g fat (1g sat. fat), 18mg chol., 87mg sod., 1g carb. (1g sugars, 0 fiber), 3g pro.

PIZZA PUFFS

❄ PIZZA PUFFS

What's more fun than a pizza puff? Skip the kind sold in the frozen aisle and try this homemade version. You can substitute any meat or vegetable for the pepperoni and any cheese for the mozzarella.
—*Vivi Taylor, Middleburg, FL*

TAKES: 30 min. • **MAKES:** 20 servings

- 1 loaf (1 lb.) frozen pizza dough, thawed
- 20 slices pepperoni
- 8 oz. part-skim mozzarella cheese, cut into 20 cubes
- ¼ cup butter
- 2 small garlic cloves, minced
  Dash salt
  Marinara sauce, warmed
  Optional: Crushed red pepper flakes and grated Parmesan cheese

1. Preheat oven to 400°. Shape dough into 1½-in. balls; flatten into ⅛-in. thick circles. Place 1 pepperoni slice and 1 cheese cube in center of each circle; wrap dough around pepperoni and cheese. Pinch edges to seal; shape into a ball. Repeat with the remaining dough, cheese and pepperoni. Place balls seam side down on greased baking sheets; bake until light golden brown, 10-15 minutes. Cool slightly.

2. Meanwhile, in a small saucepan, melt butter over low heat. Add garlic and salt, taking care not to brown butter or garlic; brush over puffs. Serve with marinara sauce; if desired, sprinkle with red pepper flakes and Parmesan.

Freeze option: Cover and freeze unbaked pizza puffs on waxed paper-lined baking sheets until firm. Transfer to a freezer container; return to freezer. To use, preheat oven to 400°; bake pizza puffs on greased baking sheets as directed, increasing time as necessary until golden brown.

1 pizza puff: 120 cal., 6g fat (3g sat. fat), 15mg chol., 189mg sod., 11g carb. (1g sugars, 0 fiber), 5g pro.

❄ CHEDDAR CORN DOG MUFFINS

I wanted a change from hot dogs, so I made corn dog muffins. I added jalapenos to this kid-friendly recipe, and that won my husband over, too.
—*Becky Tarala, Palm Coast, FL*

TAKES: 25 min. • **MAKES:** 9 muffins

- 1 pkg. (8½ oz.) cornbread/muffin mix
- ⅔ cup 2% milk
- 1 large egg, lightly beaten, room temperature
- 5 turkey hot dogs, sliced
- ½ cup shredded sharp cheddar cheese
- 2 Tbsp. finely chopped pickled jalapeno, optional

1. Preheat oven to 400°. Line 9 muffin cups with foil liners or grease 9 nonstick muffin cups.

2. In a small bowl, combine muffin mix, milk and egg; stir in hot dogs, cheese and, if desired, jalapeno. Fill the prepared cups three-fourths full.

3. Bake until a toothpick inserted in center comes out clean, 14-18 minutes. Cool for 5 minutes before removing from pan to a wire rack. Serve warm. Refrigerate leftovers.

Freeze option: Freeze cooled muffins in freezer containers. To use, microwave each muffin on high until heated through, 30-60 seconds.

1 muffin: 216 cal., 10g fat (4g sat. fat), 46mg chol., 619mg sod., 23g carb. (7g sugars, 2g fiber), 8g pro.

MAKE-AHEAD SAUSAGE PINWHEELS

❄ MAKE-AHEAD SAUSAGE PINWHEELS

Filled with sausage, sweet pepper and cream cheese, these roll-ups are excellent for unexpected visitors, a cocktail party or a halftime snack. Besides being easy to make, they can be done way ahead and kept in the freezer. All you have to do is pop them into a hot oven!
—*Cindy Nerat, Menominee, MI*

PREP: 30 min. + freezing • **BAKE:** 15 min.
MAKES: about 6½ dozen

- 1 lb. bulk regular or spicy pork sausage
- ½ cup diced sweet red pepper
- 1 green onion, chopped
- 1 pkg. (8 oz.) cream cheese, cubed
- 2 tubes (8 oz. each) refrigerated crescent rolls

1. Preheat oven to 350°. In a large skillet, cook and crumble sausage over medium-high heat until no longer pink, 5-7 minutes; drain. Add pepper and green onion; cook and stir for 2 minutes. Transfer to a bowl; cool 10 minutes. Stir in the cream cheese until blended; cool completely.

2. Unroll 1 can of crescent dough and separate into 4 rectangles; pinch perforations to seal. Press each rectangle to 6x4½ in.; spread each with ⅓ cup filling to within ¼ in. of edges. Roll up jelly-roll style, starting with a short side; pinch seam to seal. Roll gently to make logs smooth. Place on a waxed paper-lined baking sheet, seam side down. Repeat with remaining crescent dough. Freeze, covered, until firm, about 1 hour.

3. Cut each log into 10 slices. Bake on parchment-lined baking sheets until golden brown, 15-18 minutes. Serve warm.

Freeze option: Freeze pinwheels in freezer containers, separating layers with waxed paper. To use, bake frozen pinwheels as directed, increasing time by 3-5 minutes.

1 appetizer: 46 cal., 3g fat (1g sat. fat), 6mg chol., 89mg sod., 2g carb. (1g sugars, 0 fiber), 1g pro.

BUFFALO CHICKEN SLIDERS

I came up with the idea for these sliders from my mom and dad, who'd made a similar recipe for a family get-together. To make it special, I sometimes use several different styles of buffalo sauce and let guests mix and match their favorites.

—*Christina Addison, Blanchester, OH*

- -

PREP: 20 min. • **COOK:** 3 hours
MAKES: 6 servings

- 1   lb. boneless skinless chicken breasts
- 2   Tbsp. plus ⅓ cup Louisiana-style hot sauce, divided
- ¼   tsp. pepper
- ¼   cup butter, cubed
- ¼   cup honey
- 12 Hawaiian sweet rolls, warmed
     Optional: Lettuce leaves, sliced tomato, thinly sliced red onion and crumbled blue cheese

1. Place chicken in a 3-qt. slow cooker. Toss with 2 Tbsp. hot sauce and the pepper; cook, covered, on low 3-4 hours or until tender.
2. Remove chicken; discard cooking juices. In a small saucepan, combine butter, honey and the remaining ⅓ cup hot sauce; cook and stir over medium heat until blended.
3. Shred chicken with 2 forks; stir into sauce and heat through. Serve on rolls with desired optional ingredients.
Freeze option: Freeze cooled chicken mixture in freezer containers. To use, partially thaw in refrigerator overnight. Microwave, covered, on high in a microwave-safe dish until heated through, stirring occasionally; add water or broth if necessary.
2 sliders: 396 cal., 15g fat (8g sat. fat), 92mg chol., 873mg sod., 44g carb. (24g sugars, 2g fiber), 24g pro.

SLOW-COOKED PEACH SALSA

Fresh peaches and tomatoes make my salsa a hands-down winner over store versions. As a treat, I give my co-workers several jars throughout the year.

—*Peggi Stahnke, Cleveland, OH*

- -

PREP: 20 min. • **COOK:** 3 hours + cooling
MAKES: 11 cups

- 4   lbs. tomatoes (about 12 medium), chopped
- 1   medium onion, chopped
- 4   jalapeno peppers, seeded and finely chopped
- ½   to ⅔ cup packed brown sugar
- ¼   cup minced fresh cilantro
- 4   garlic cloves, minced
- 1   tsp. salt
- 4   cups chopped peeled fresh peaches (about 4 medium), divided
- 1   can (6 oz.) tomato paste

1. In a 5-qt. slow cooker, combine the first 7 ingredients; stir in 2 cups peaches. Cook, covered, on low 3-4 hours or until the onion is tender.
2. Stir tomato paste and remaining 2 cups peaches into the slow cooker. Cool. Transfer to covered containers. Refrigerate up to 1 week.
Freeze option: Fill freezer-safe containers to within ½ in. of tops. Freeze up to 12 months. Thaw in refrigerator before serving.
Note: Wear disposable gloves when cutting hot peppers; the oils can burn skin. Avoid touching your face.
¼ cup: 28 cal., 0 fat (0 sat. fat), 0 chol., 59mg sod., 7g carb. (5g sugars, 1g fiber), 1g pro.
Diabetic exchanges: ½ starch.

BUFFALO CHICKEN SLIDERS

MEDITERRANEAN
VEGGIE BRUNCH
PUFF, P. 24

Breakfast & Brunch

A pull-out-all-the-stops breakfast doesn't mean getting up at the crack of dawn! These recipes let you treat your guests *and* sleep in!

FLUFFY BANANA
PANCAKES, P. 25

OVERNIGHT EGG CASSEROLE

This is my go-to breakfast dish when hosting overnight guests. Because it is prepared the night before, all you have to do is pop it in the oven in the morning.

—*LaVonne Propst, Sweet Home, OR*

- -

PREP: 15 min. + chilling • **BAKE:** 50 min.
MAKES: 8 servings

8	slices bread, cubed
¾	lb. shredded cheddar cheese
1½	lbs. bulk pork sausage or Italian sausage
4	large eggs
2½	cups 2% milk
1	Tbsp. prepared mustard
1	can (10¾ oz.) condensed cream of mushroom soup, undiluted
¼	cup chicken broth

1. Place bread cubes in a greased 13x9-in. baking dish. Sprinkle with cheese; set aside. In a skillet, cook sausage over medium heat until no longer pink; drain. Crumble sausage over the cheese and bread. Beat the eggs, milk, mustard, soup and broth; pour over the sausage. Refrigerate, covered, at least 2-3 hours or overnight.

2. Remove from the refrigerator 30 minutes before baking. Bake, uncovered, at 350° for 50-60 minutes or just until set. Let stand for 5 minutes before cutting.

1 serving: 526 cal., 38g fat (18g sat. fat), 194mg chol., 1134mg sod., 21g carb. (7g sugars, 1g fiber), 25g pro.

❄ FREEZER BREAKFAST SANDWICHES

On a busy morning, these freezer breakfast sandwiches save the day. A hearty combo of eggs, Canadian bacon and cheese will keep you fueled through lunchtime and beyond.

—*Christine Rukavena, Milwaukee, WI*

- -

PREP: 25 min. • **COOK:** 15 min.
MAKES: 12 sandwiches

12	large eggs
⅔	cup 2% milk
½	tsp. salt
¼	tsp. pepper

SANDWICHES

12	English muffins, split
4	Tbsp. butter, softened
12	slices Colby-Monterey Jack cheese
12	slices Canadian bacon

1. Preheat oven to 325°. In a large bowl, whisk eggs, milk, salt and pepper until blended. Pour into a 13x9-in. baking pan coated with cooking spray. Bake until set, 15-18 minutes. Cool on a wire rack.

2. Meanwhile, toast English muffins (or bake at 325° until lightly browned, 12-15 minutes). Spread 1 tsp. butter on each muffin bottom.

3. Cut eggs into 12 portions. Layer muffin bottoms with an egg portion, a cheese slice (tearing cheese to fit) and Canadian bacon. Replace muffin tops. Wrap in waxed paper and then foil; freeze in a freezer container.

To use frozen sandwiches: Remove foil. Microwave a waxed paper-wrapped sandwich at 50% power until thawed, 1-2 minutes. Turn sandwich over; microwave at 100% power until hot and a thermometer reads at least 160°, 30-60 seconds. Let stand 2 minutes before serving.

1 sandwich: 334 cal., 17g fat (9g sat. fat), 219mg chol., 759mg sod., 26g carb. (3g sugars, 2g fiber), 19g pro.

FREEZER BREAKFAST SANDWICHES

FRENCH TOAST
STICKS

OVERNIGHT HAM & EGG CASSEROLE

I love how easy it is to assemble this savory egg casserole. Putting it together the night before really frees up my time the next morning.
—*Jennifer Howell, Fort Collins, CO*

- -

PREP: 10 min. + chilling • **BAKE:** 1 hour
MAKES: 9 servings

  4   **cups frozen shredded hash brown potatoes, thawed**
  1   **cup cubed fully cooked ham**
  1   **can (4 oz.) chopped green chiles**
 ½   **cup shredded Monterey Jack cheese**
 ½   **cup shredded cheddar cheese**
  6   **large eggs**
  1   **can (12 oz.) evaporated milk**
 ¼   **tsp. pepper**
     Salsa, optional

1. In a greased 8-in. square baking dish, layer the hash browns, ham, chiles and cheeses. In a large bowl, whisk the eggs, milk and pepper; pour over casserole. Refrigerate, covered, overnight.
2. Remove from the refrigerator 30 minutes before baking. Preheat oven to 350°. Bake, uncovered, until a knife inserted in center comes out clean, about 1 hour. Let stand 5-10 minutes. Serve with salsa if desired.
1 piece: 203 cal., 11g fat (6g sat. fat), 175mg chol., 407mg sod., 11g carb. (5g sugars, 1g fiber), 14g pro. **Diabetic exchanges:** 2 lean meat, ½ starch, ½ fat.

❄ FRENCH TOAST STICKS

Keep these French toast sticks in the freezer for an instant filling breakfast. Their convenient size makes them ideal for a breakfast buffet.
—*Taste of Home Test Kitchen*

- -

PREP: 20 min. + freezing • **BAKE:** 20 min.
MAKES: 1½ dozen

  6   **slices day-old Texas toast**
  4   **large eggs**
  1   **cup 2% milk**
  2   **Tbsp. sugar**
  1   **tsp. vanilla extract**
 ¼   **to ½ tsp. ground cinnamon**
  1   **cup crushed cornflakes, optional**
     Confectioners' sugar, optional
     Maple syrup

1. Cut each piece of bread into thirds; place in a single layer in an ungreased 13x9-in. dish. In a large bowl, whisk the eggs, milk, sugar, vanilla and cinnamon. Pour over bread; soak for 2 minutes, turning once. If desired, coat bread with cornflake crumbs on all sides.
2. Place in a greased 15x10x1-in. baking pan. Freeze until firm, about 45 minutes. Transfer to an airtight freezer container and store in the freezer.
To use frozen French toast sticks: Place desired number on a greased baking sheet. Bake at 425° for 8 minutes. Turn; bake 10-12 minutes longer or until golden brown. Sprinkle with confectioners' sugar if desired. Serve with syrup.
3 sticks: 183 cal., 6g fat (2g sat. fat), 145mg chol., 251mg sod., 24g carb. (8g sugars, 1g fiber), 8g pro.

CREAMY STRAWBERRY FRENCH TOAST BAKE

On Sunday mornings I like to take it easy, but I still want my family to have a nice breakfast. This recipe allows me to sleep in but still feel as if I'm a fabulous mom. Win!
—*Alynn Hansen, Mona, UT*

PREP: 30 min. + chilling • **BAKE:** 40 min.
MAKES: 8 servings

- 3 cups sliced fresh strawberries, divided
- 2 Tbsp. sugar
- 1 pkg. (8 oz.) cream cheese, softened
- ½ cup confectioners' sugar
- 1 Tbsp. grated orange zest
- 1 Tbsp. orange juice
- 1 tsp. vanilla extract
- 1 loaf (1 lb.) cinnamon bread, cut into 1-in. pieces
- 5 large eggs
- 1 cup half-and-half cream
  Sweetened whipped cream

1. Toss 2 cups strawberries with sugar. In another bowl, beat the next 5 ingredients until smooth. Place half the bread in a greased 13x9-in. baking dish. Spoon cream cheese mixture over bread. Layer with strawberry mixture and remaining bread. Whisk the eggs and cream until blended; pour over top. Refrigerate, covered, overnight.
2. Preheat oven to 350°. Remove casserole from refrigerator while oven heats. Bake, uncovered, until a knife inserted in the center comes out clean, 40-45 minutes. Let stand 5 minutes before serving. Top with whipped cream and remaining 1 cup strawberries.
1 piece: 431 cal., 21g fat (10g sat. fat), 160mg chol., 382mg sod., 47g carb. (24g sugars, 5g fiber), 13g pro.

> **TEST KITCHEN TIP**
> Once you've made this bake, try it with other berries and flavors as well. The combination of blueberries and lemon would be delicious here!

BACON SWISS QUICHE

❄ BACON SWISS QUICHE

With a quiche like this, you don't need a lot of heavy side dishes. It's got everything—eggs, bacon, cheese and a touch of apple juice for a salty-sweet fix.
—*Colleen Belbey, Warwick, RI*

PREP: 15 min.
BAKE: 40 min. + standing
MAKES: 6 servings

- 1 sheet refrigerated pie crust
- ¼ cup sliced green onions
- 1 Tbsp. butter
- 6 large eggs
- 1½ cups heavy whipping cream
- ¼ cup unsweetened apple juice
- 1 lb. sliced bacon, cooked and crumbled
- ⅛ tsp. salt
- ⅛ tsp. pepper
- 2 cups shredded Swiss cheese

1. Preheat oven to 350°. Line a 9-in. pie plate with crust; trim and flute edges. Set aside. In a small skillet, saute green onions in butter until tender. In a large bowl, whisk eggs, cream and juice. Stir in bacon, salt, pepper and green onions. Pour into crust; sprinkle with cheese.
2. Bake until a knife inserted in the center comes out clean, 40-45 minutes. Let stand 10 minutes before cutting.
Freeze option: Securely wrap individual portions of cooled quiche in parchment and foil; freeze. To use, partially thaw in refrigerator overnight. Remove from refrigerator 30 minutes before baking. Preheat oven to 350°. Unwrap the quiche; reheat in oven until heated through and a thermometer inserted in center reads 165°.
1 piece: 739 cal., 60g fat (31g sat. fat), 359mg chol., 781mg sod., 22g carb. (4g sugars, 0 fiber), 27g pro.
Ham Quiche: Omit apple juice. Increase cream to 1¾ cup. Substitute 3 cups diced cooked ham for the bacon, and cheddar cheese for the Swiss cheese. Proceed as directed.
Ham Broccoli Quiche: Follow directions for the Ham Quiche. Add 1 cup chopped broccoli florets to the egg mixture.

❄ WHOLE WHEAT PECAN WAFFLES

We bought a new waffle maker, and a recipe came along with it. We finally tried it, and after a few changes to suit our tastes, these amazing waffles were the result.
—*Sarah Morris, Joplin, MO*

TAKES: 30 min. • **MAKES:** 16 waffles

- 2 **cups whole wheat pastry flour**
- 2 **Tbsp. sugar**
- 3 **tsp. baking powder**
- ½ **tsp. salt**
- 2 **large eggs, separated, room temperature**
- 1¾ **cups fat-free milk**
- ¼ **cup canola oil**
- ½ **cup chopped pecans**

1. Preheat waffle maker. Whisk together the first 4 ingredients. In another bowl, whisk together egg yolks, milk and oil; add to flour mixture, stirring just until moistened.
2. In a clean bowl, beat egg whites on medium speed until stiff but not dry. Fold into batter. Cook waffles according to manufacturer's directions until golden brown, sprinkling batter with pecans after pouring.
Freeze option: Cool waffles on wire racks. Freeze between layers of waxed paper in a freezer container. Reheat waffles in a toaster or toaster oven on medium setting.
2 waffles (4 in.): 241 cal., 14g fat (1g sat. fat), 48mg chol., 338mg sod., 24g carb. (6g sugars, 3g fiber), 7g pro. **Diabetic exchanges:** 2½ fat, 1½ starch.

BROCCOLI & CHICKEN CHEESE STRATA

On our dairy farm, chores often delay dinner. That's when this strata comes in handy. I'll prepare it beforehand and later load it in the oven for a quick and easy meal.
—*Margery Moore, Richfield Springs, NY*

PREP: 15 min. + chilling
BAKE: 1 hour + standing • **MAKES:** 8 servings

- 12 **slices bread**
- 2¼ **cups shredded cheddar cheese, divided**
- 3 **cups frozen chopped broccoli, thawed and drained**
- 2 **cups diced cooked chicken**
- 1 **Tbsp. butter, melted**
- 6 **large eggs**
- 3 **cups 2% milk**
- 2 **Tbsp. finely chopped onion**
- ¾ **tsp. salt**
- ½ **tsp. ground mustard**
- ¼ **tsp. pepper**

1. Using a doughnut cutter, cut 12 rings and holes in bread; set aside. Tear the remaining bread scraps and place in a greased 13x9-in. baking dish. Sprinkle with 2 cups cheese, the broccoli and chicken. Arrange bread rings and holes on top; brush with melted butter.
2. Beat next 6 ingredients; pour over top. Refrigerate, covered, 8 hours or overnight.
3. Remove strata from refrigerator 30 minutes before baking. Preheat oven to 325°. Bake, uncovered, 55-60 minutes. Sprinkle with remaining ¼ cup cheese; bake until a knife inserted in center comes out clean, about 5 minutes longer. Let stand for 5-10 minutes before cutting.
1 piece: 440 cal., 22g fat (10g sat. fat), 213mg chol., 794mg sod., 30g carb. (8g sugars, 3g fiber), 31g pro.

BROCCOLI & CHICKEN CHEESE STRATA

OVERNIGHT BAKED EGGS BRUSCHETTA

I like to spend as much time as I can with my guests when they stay with me for the holidays, so I rely on make-ahead recipes to help that happen. Because most overnight brunch casseroles are so similar, I came up with a breakfast bruschetta for a fun change of pace.

—*Judi Berman-Yamada, Portland, OR*

- -

PREP: 45 min. + chilling • **BAKE:** 10 min.
MAKES: 9 servings

- 1 tube (13.8 oz.) refrigerated pizza crust
- 1 Tbsp. cornmeal
- 3 Tbsp. olive oil, divided
- 1½ cups shredded part-skim mozzarella cheese, divided
- ¾ lb. sliced baby portobello mushrooms
- ¾ tsp. garlic powder
- ¾ tsp. dried rosemary, crushed
- ½ tsp. pepper
- ¼ tsp. salt
- 2 cups pizza sauce
- 1 Tbsp. white vinegar
- 9 large eggs
- 2 oz. fresh goat cheese, crumbled
- ½ cup french-fried onions
  Fresh basil leaves

1. Preheat oven to 400°. Unroll the pizza crust and press onto bottom of a greased 15x10x1-in. baking pan that's been sprinkled with cornmeal. Brush crust with 1 Tbsp. oil; sprinkle with ¾ cup mozzarella cheese. Bake 8 minutes.

2. Meanwhile, in a large skillet, heat remaining oil over medium-high heat. Add mushrooms; cook and stir until tender. Stir in garlic powder, rosemary and seasonings. Stir pizza sauce into mushrooms; spread mushroom mixture over crust.

3. In a large skillet with high sides, bring vinegar and 2-3 in. water to a boil. Reduce heat to maintain a gentle simmer. Break cold eggs, 1 at a time, into a small bowl; holding bowl close to surface of water, slip eggs into water.

4. Cook, uncovered, 3-5 minutes or until whites are completely set and yolks begin to thicken but are not hard. Using a slotted spoon, remove eggs; place over mushrooms in baking pan. Sprinkle the goat cheese and remaining mozzarella over eggs and mushrooms. Refrigerate, covered, overnight.

5. Remove pan from refrigerator 30 minutes before baking. Preheat oven to 400°. Sprinkle onions over top. Bake, uncovered, until golden brown and heated through, 10-15 minutes. Top with basil just before serving.

1 piece: 345 cal., 17g fat (5g sat. fat), 227mg chol., 798mg sod., 29g carb. (6g sugars, 2g fiber), 17g pro.

OVERNIGHT SAUSAGE & GRITS

This recipe is so appealing because you can make it the night before and then put it in the oven an hour before you want to eat. It works well as a side with pancakes or waffles, but you can also make it the main course for brunch events.

—*Susan Ham, Cleveland, TN*

- -

PREP: 10 min. + chilling
BAKE: 1 hour • **MAKES:** 12 servings

- 3 cups hot cooked grits
- 2½ cups shredded cheddar cheese
- 1 lb. bulk pork sausage, cooked and crumbled
- 3 large eggs
- 1½ cups 2% milk
- 3 Tbsp. butter, melted
- ¼ tsp. garlic powder

1. Mix grits, cheese and sausage. Beat eggs and milk; stir into the grits. Add butter and garlic powder. Transfer to a greased 13x9-in. baking dish. Refrigerate, covered, for 8 hours or overnight.

2. Remove dish from refrigerator 30 minutes before baking. Preheat oven to 350°. Bake, uncovered, until a knife inserted in center comes out clean, about 1 hour. Let stand 5 minutes before cutting.

1 piece: 259 cal., 19g fat (10g sat. fat), 104mg chol., 491mg sod., 11g carb. (2g sugars, 0 fiber), 11g pro.

OVERNIGHT BAKED EGGS BRUSCHETTA

HOMEMADE BREAKFAST
SASAGE PATTIES

❄️
HOMEMADE BREAKFAST SAUSAGE PATTIES

Buttermilk is the secret ingredient that keeps these pork patties moist, while a blend of seasonings creates a wonderful taste.
—*Harvey Keeney, Mandan, ND*

- -

PREP: 30 min. • **COOK:** 10 min./batch
MAKES: 20 patties

¾	cup buttermilk
2¼	tsp. kosher salt
1½	tsp. rubbed sage
1½	tsp. brown sugar
1½	tsp. pepper
¾	tsp. dried marjoram
¾	tsp. dried savory
¾	tsp. cayenne pepper
¼	tsp. ground nutmeg
2½	lbs. ground pork

1. In a large bowl, combine first 9 ingredients. Add pork; mix lightly but thoroughly. Shape into twenty 3-in. patties.

2. In a large skillet coated with cooking spray, cook patties in batches over medium heat until a thermometer reads 160°, 5-6 minutes on each side. Remove to paper towels to drain.

Freeze option: Wrap each cooked, cooled patty; transfer to an airtight container. Freeze for up to 3 months. To use, unwrap patties and place on a baking sheet coated with cooking spray. Bake at 350° until heated through, about 15 minutes on each side.

Note: To substitute for each cup of buttermilk, use 1 Tbsp. white vinegar or lemon juice plus enough milk to measure 1 cup. Stir, then let stand 5 minutes. Or use 1 cup plain yogurt or 1¾ tsp. cream of tartar plus 1 cup milk.

1 patty: 126 cal., 8g fat (3g sat. fat), 38mg chol., 251mg sod., 1g carb. (1g sugars, 0 fiber), 11g pro.

CHICKEN CHILES RELLENOS STRATA

This versatile bake can be made as an entree, a brunch option or a potluck dish. It's one of the easiest meals to assemble on a busy weeknight.
—*Kallee Krong-McCreery, Escondido, CA*

- -

PREP: 20 min. + chilling
BAKE: 35 min. + standing • **MAKES:** 10 servings

    6 cups cubed French bread (about 6 oz.)
    2 cans (4 oz. each) chopped green chiles
    2 cups shredded Monterey Jack cheese
    2 cups shredded cooked chicken
   12 large eggs
 1½ cups 2% milk
    2 tsp. baking powder
    1 tsp. garlic salt
    1 cup shredded cheddar cheese
       Salsa

1. In a greased 13x9-in. baking dish, layer half each of the following: bread cubes, chiles, Monterey Jack cheese and chicken. Repeat the layers.
2. In a large bowl, whisk eggs, milk, baking powder and garlic salt until blended. Pour over layers. Sprinkle with cheddar cheese. Refrigerate, covered, overnight.
3. Preheat oven to 350°. Remove strata from refrigerator while oven heats. Bake, uncovered, 35-40 minutes or until puffed and golden at edges. Let stand 10 minutes before serving. Serve with salsa.
1 piece: 338 cal., 20g fat (9g sat. fat), 282mg chol., 820mg sod., 13g carb. (3g sugars, 1g fiber), 27g pro.

TEST KITCHEN TIP
You can vary the cheese in this recipe. Look for a solid, semi-soft white cheese with a mild flavor that melts well. Try pepper jack or colby jack, or a Mexican quesillo.

CHICKEN CHILES
RELLENOS STRATA

OVERNIGHT BAKED OATMEAL

My husband and I spent a long weekend at a bed-and-breakfast not far from our home. The owners shared this delicious recipe with me, which I made my own after a couple of simple changes.
—*Jennifer Cramer, Lebanon, PA*

PREP: 10 min. + chilling • **BAKE:** 40 min.
MAKES: 8 servings

- 2 large eggs, room temperature, lightly beaten
- 3 cups 2% milk
- ¾ cup packed brown sugar
- ¼ cup canola oil
- 1½ tsp. ground cinnamon
- 1 tsp. salt
- 2 cups old-fashioned oats
- ¼ cup dried blueberries
- ¼ cup dried cherries
- ¼ cup sliced almonds

1. In a large bowl, whisk together the first 6 ingredients. Stir in the oats, blueberries and cherries. Transfer to a greased 8-in. square baking dish. Refrigerate, covered, 8 hours or overnight.
2. Preheat oven to 350°. Remove oatmeal from refrigerator while oven heats. Stir oatmeal; sprinkle with almonds. Bake, uncovered, until golden brown and a thermometer reads 160°, 40-50 minutes. Serve warm.
½ cup: 331 cal., 13g fat (2g sat. fat), 54mg chol., 364mg sod., 46g carb. (30g sugars, 4g fiber), 8g pro.

❄ MEDITERRANEAN VEGGIE BRUNCH PUFF

I make breakfast casseroles with whatever I have on hand, and that's often spinach, sweet red pepper and cheddar. I like to give this puff a burst of flavor with a spoonful of Greek vinaigrette topping.
—*Angela Robinson, Findlay, OH*

PREP: 25 min. + chilling • **BAKE:** 25 min.
MAKES: 8 servings

- 6 large eggs
- 2 large egg whites
- 1 cup 2% milk
- 1 garlic clove, minced
- ½ tsp. salt
- ¼ tsp. pepper
- 5 cups cubed croissants (about 6 oz.)
- ¾ cup chopped roasted sweet red peppers, divided
- ½ cup finely chopped sweet onion
- 1 pkg. (10 oz.) frozen chopped spinach, thawed and squeezed dry
- 1 cup shredded cheddar cheese
- ½ cup crumbled feta cheese
- 3 Tbsp. Greek vinaigrette

1. In a large bowl, whisk the first 6 ingredients until blended. Place croissant pieces in a single layer in a greased 11x7-in. baking dish; top with ½ cup red pepper, onion and spinach. Pour egg mixture over top. Sprinkle with cheeses. Refrigerate, covered, overnight.
2. Finely chop remaining ¼ cup chopped red pepper; place in a jar with a tight-fitting lid. Add vinaigrette; shake to combine and refrigerate until serving.
3. Preheat oven to 350°. Remove casserole from refrigerator while oven heats. Bake, uncovered, 25-30 minutes or until a knife inserted in the center comes out clean. Let stand 5-10 minutes before cutting. Serve with the vinaigrette mixture.
Freeze option: Cover and freeze unbaked casserole and remaining chopped sweet red pepper separately. To use, partially thaw both in refrigerator overnight. Remove 30 minutes before baking. Bake the casserole at 350° as directed, increasing time as necessary to heat through and for a thermometer inserted in center to read 165°. Finely chop remaining sweet red pepper; combine with vinaigrette as directed and serve with the casserole.
1 piece with 1½ tsp. vinaigrette: 281 cal., 17g fat (8g sat. fat), 175mg chol., 656mg sod., 16g carb. (6g sugars, 2g fiber), 14g pro.

MEDITERRANEAN VEGGIE BRUNCH PUFF

FLUFFY BANANA PANCAKES

HAWAIIAN HAM STRATA

I came up with this recipe because I love Hawaiian pizza and wanted a casserole I could make ahead and pop in the oven at the last minute. This is a perfect main dish to take to a potluck.
—*Lisa Renshaw, Kansas City, MO*

- -

PREP: 20 min. + chilling
COOK: 30 min. + standing • **MAKES:** 8 servings

  8 **English muffins,**
      cut into eighths and toasted
  3 **cups cubed fully cooked ham**
  1 **can (20 oz.) pineapple tidbits, drained**
  4 **green onions, chopped**
  1 **jar (4 oz.) diced pimientos, drained**
1½ **cups shredded cheddar cheese**
 ¼ **cup grated Parmesan cheese**
  1 **jar (15 oz.) Alfredo sauce**
1½ **cups evaporated milk**
  4 **large eggs, lightly beaten**
 ½ **tsp. salt**
 ¼ **tsp. cayenne pepper**

1. Combine the first 5 ingredients. Transfer to a 13x9-in. baking dish; top with cheeses.
2. Whisk together remaining ingredients. Pour sauce over layers, pushing down, if necessary, with the back of a spoon to ensure the muffins absorb the liquid. Refrigerate, covered, 1 hour or overnight.
3. Preheat oven to 350°. Remove strata from refrigerator while oven heats. Bake, uncovered, until the strata is golden and bubbly, 30-40 minutes. Let stand 10 minutes before serving.
1 piece: 515 cal., 22g fat (12g sat. fat), 177mg chol., 1512mg sod., 48g carb. (16g sugars, 3g fiber), 31g pro.

❄ FLUFFY BANANA PANCAKES

I love to make pancakes for my family on Saturday mornings. Since we often have ripe bananas, I decided to add them to a batch of pancake batter. The results were marvelous!
—*Lori Stevens, Riverton, UT*

- -

TAKES: 30 min. • **MAKES:** 7 servings

  1 **cup all-purpose flour**
  1 **cup whole wheat flour**
  3 **Tbsp. brown sugar**
  1 **tsp. baking powder**
  1 **tsp. baking soda**
  1 **tsp. ground cinnamon**
 ½ **tsp. salt**
  2 **large eggs, room temperature**
  2 **cups buttermilk**
  2 **Tbsp. canola oil**
  1 **tsp. vanilla extract**
  1 **ripe medium banana, finely chopped**
 ⅓ **cup finely chopped walnuts**

1. In a large bowl, combine the first 7 ingredients. In another bowl, whisk eggs, buttermilk, oil and vanilla until blended. Add to the dry ingredients, stirring just until moistened. Fold in banana and walnuts.
2. Pour batter by ¼ cupfuls onto a hot griddle coated with cooking spray. Cook until bubbles begin to form on top and bottoms are golden brown. Turn; cook until the second side is golden brown.
Freeze option: Freeze cooled pancakes between layers of waxed paper in a freezer container. To use, place pancakes on an ungreased baking sheet, cover with foil and reheat in a preheated 375° oven for 5-10 minutes. Or place 2 pancakes on a microwave-safe plate and microwave on high for 40-50 seconds or until heated through.
2 pancakes: 283 cal., 10g fat (2g sat. fat), 63mg chol., 503mg sod., 40g carb. (12g sugars, 4g fiber), 9g pro. **Diabetic exchanges:** 2½ starch, 1½ fat.
Fluffy Strawberry Pancakes: Replace chopped banana with ¾ cup chopped fresh strawberries; proceed as directed.
Fluffy Peach Pancakes: Replace chopped banana with ¾ cup chopped fresh or frozen peaches; proceed as directed.
Fluffy Blueberry Pancakes: Replace chopped banana with ¾ cup chopped fresh or frozen blueberries; proceed as directed.

Soups, Stews & Chilis

For make-ahead convenience, these recipes offer deliciously easy options.

ROASTED CAULIFLOWER
& RED PEPPER SOUP, P. 35

PIZZA SOUP WITH
GARLIC TOAST
CROUTONS, P. 32

❄ SATISFYING TOMATO SOUP

After craving tomato soup, I decided to make my own. Mine is smooth but my sister Joan prefers it chunky, so she doesn't puree. Serve it with a grilled cheese sandwich on the side.
—*Marian Brown, Mississauga, ON*

- -

TAKES: 30 min. • **MAKES:** 4 servings

- 2 tsp. canola oil
- ¼ cup finely chopped onion
- ¼ cup finely chopped celery
- 2 cans (14½ oz. each) diced tomatoes, undrained
- 1½ cups water
- 2 tsp. brown sugar
- ½ tsp. salt
- ½ tsp. dried basil
- ¼ tsp. dried oregano
- ¼ tsp. coarsely ground pepper
  Minced fresh basil, optional

1. In a large saucepan, heat oil over medium-high heat. Add onion and celery; cook and stir until tender, 2-4 minutes. Add remaining ingredients except optional fresh basil. Bring to a boil. Reduce heat; simmer, uncovered, 10 minutes to allow flavors to blend.

2. Puree soup using an immersion blender. Or cool soup slightly and puree in batches in a blender; return to pan and heat through. If desired, top with fresh minced basil.

Freeze option: Freeze cooled soup in freezer containers. To use, partially thaw in refrigerator overnight. Heat through in a saucepan, stirring occasionally; add water if necessary.

1¼ cups: 76 cal., 2g fat (0 sat. fat), 0 chol., 627mg sod., 13g carb. (9g sugars, 4g fiber), 2g pro. **Diabetic exchanges:** 2 vegetable, ½ fat.

TEST KITCHEN TIP

For grilled cheese "croutons" that won't immediately soak up all the soup, use day-old bread and low heat so you end up with a crispy, drier sandwich. Butter 1 side of 2 slices of day-old, hearty bread. Place 1 slice, butter side down, in a skillet over medium-low heat; top with your favorite cheese slices. Top with the second slice, butter side up, and cook until dark golden brown, 4-5 minutes. Flip and cook another 4-5 minutes. Remove and cut into cubes.

SIMPLE ASPARAGUS SOUP

❄ SIMPLE ASPARAGUS SOUP

My family and friends love this soup and think I spend hours making it, but the most time spent is on occasional stirring.
—*Kathryn Labat, Raceland, LA*

- -

PREP: 20 min. • **COOK:** 55 min.
MAKES: 12 servings (2¼ qt.)

- 1 Tbsp. butter
- 1 Tbsp. olive oil
- 2 lbs. fresh asparagus, trimmed and cut into 1-in. pieces
- 1 medium onion, chopped
- 1 medium carrot, thinly sliced
- ½ tsp. salt
- ¼ tsp. pepper
- ¼ tsp. dried thyme
- ⅔ cup uncooked long grain brown rice
- 6 cups reduced-sodium chicken broth
  Optional: Reduced-fat sour cream and salad croutons

1. In a 6-qt. stockpot, heat butter and oil over medium heat. Stir in vegetables and seasonings; cook until vegetables are tender, 8-10 minutes, stirring occasionally.

2. Stir in rice and broth; bring to a boil. Reduce heat; simmer, covered, until rice is tender, 40-45 minutes, stirring occasionally.

3. Puree soup using an immersion blender, or cool slightly and puree soup in batches in a blender. Return to pot and heat through. If desired, serve with sour cream and croutons.

Freeze option: Freeze cooled soup in freezer containers. When ready to use, partially thaw in refrigerator overnight (soup may separate). In a saucepan, reheat to boiling, whisking until blended.

¾ cup: 79 cal., 3g fat (1g sat. fat), 3mg chol., 401mg sod., 11g carb. (2g sugars, 2g fiber), 4g pro. **Diabetic exchanges:** 1 vegetable, ½ starch, ½ fat.

❄ 🍲 BRAZILIAN STEW

During high school, I spent a year in Brazil and fell in love with the culture and the food. One of my favorite dishes was feijoada, a chili/stew served over white rice. I introduced this easy recipe to my family and it has become one of our favorite comfort foods.

—*Andrea Romanczyk, Magna, UT*

- -

PREP: 15 min. + soaking • **COOK:** 7 hours
MAKES: 8 servings

1½ cups dried black beans
1 lb. smoked kielbasa or Polish sausage, sliced
1 lb. boneless country-style pork ribs
1 pkg. (12 oz.) fully cooked Spanish chorizo links, sliced
1 smoked ham hock
1 large onion, chopped
3 garlic cloves, minced
2 bay leaves
¾ tsp. salt
½ tsp. pepper
5 cups water
Hot cooked rice

1. Rinse and sort beans; soak according to package directions. Drain and rinse, discarding soaking liquid.
2. In a 6-qt. slow cooker, combine beans with the next 9 ingredients. Add water; cook, covered, on low until meat and beans are tender, 7-9 hours.
3. Remove pork ribs and ham hock. When cool enough to handle, remove meat from bones; discard bones and bay leaves. Shred meat with 2 forks; return to slow cooker. Serve with hot cooked rice.

Freeze option: Freeze cooled stew in freezer containers. To use, partially thaw overnight in refrigerator. Heat through in a saucepan, stirring occasionally; add water if necessary.

1½ cups: 531 cal., 33g fat (11g sat. fat), 101mg chol., 1069mg sod., 27g carb. (3g sugars, 6g fiber), 33g pro.

BRAZILIAN STEW

❄ CHICKEN BUTTERNUT CHILI

At our house, we just love a comforting, hearty, tomato-based chili with bold flavors! This chili is loaded with veggies and flavor. You can also prepare the recipe in the slow cooker. Just add the ingredients to the crock and cook over high heat for about 4 hours.

—*Courtney Stultz, Weir, KS*

- -

PREP: 20 min. • **COOK:** 35 min.
MAKES: 4 servings

1 Tbsp. canola oil
2 medium carrots, chopped
2 celery ribs, chopped
1 medium onion, chopped
2 cups cubed peeled butternut squash
1 medium tomato, chopped
2 Tbsp. tomato paste
1 envelope reduced-sodium chili seasoning mix
2 cups chicken stock
1 cup cubed cooked chicken breast
Chopped fresh cilantro

1. In a large saucepan, heat oil over medium heat; saute carrots, celery and onion until tender, 6-8 minutes.
2. Stir in squash, tomato, tomato paste, seasoning mix and stock; bring to a boil. Reduce heat; simmer, covered, until squash is tender, 20-25 minutes. Stir in chicken; heat through. Sprinkle with cilantro.

Freeze option: Freeze cooled chili in freezer containers. To use, partially thaw in refrigerator overnight. Heat through in a saucepan, stirring occasionally.

1¼ cups: 201 cal., 5g fat (1g sat. fat), 27mg chol., 591mg sod., 25g carb. (8g sugars, 4g fiber), 15g pro. **Diabetic exchanges:** 2 lean meat, 1 starch, 1 vegetable, ½ fat.

SLOW-COOKED CHICKEN
ENCHILADA SOUP

SLOW-COOKED CHICKEN ENCHILADA SOUP

This zesty soup delivers a big bowl of comfort. Toppings such as sour cream, avocado and tortilla strips are a must.
—*Heather Sewell, Harrisonville, MO*

PREP: 25 min. • **COOK:** 6 hours
MAKES: 8 servings (3¼ qt.)

- 1   Tbsp. canola oil
- 2   Anaheim or poblano peppers, finely chopped
- 1   medium onion, chopped
- 3   garlic cloves, minced
- 1   lb. boneless skinless chicken breasts
- 1   carton (48 oz.) chicken broth
- 1   can (14½ oz.) Mexican diced tomatoes, undrained
- 1   can (10 oz.) enchilada sauce
- 2   Tbsp. tomato paste
- 1   Tbsp. chili powder
- 2   tsp. ground cumin
- ½   tsp. pepper
- ½   to 1 tsp. chipotle hot pepper sauce, optional
- ⅓   cup minced fresh cilantro
      Optional toppings: Shredded cheddar cheese, cubed avocado, sour cream and crispy tortilla strips

1. In a large skillet, heat oil over medium heat. Add peppers and onion; cook and stir until tender, 6-8 minutes. Add garlic; cook 1 minute longer. Transfer pepper mixture and chicken to a 5- or 6-qt. slow cooker. Stir in broth, tomatoes, enchilada sauce, tomato paste, seasonings and, if desired, pepper sauce. Cook, covered, on low 6-8 hours or until chicken is tender (a thermometer should read at least 165°).
2. Remove chicken from slow cooker. Shred with 2 forks; return to slow cooker. Stir in cilantro. Serve with toppings as desired.
Freeze option: Freeze cooled soup in freezer containers. To use, partially thaw in refrigerator overnight. Heat through in a saucepan, stirring occasionally; add water if necessary.
1½ cups: 125 cal., 4g fat (1g sat. fat), 35mg chol., 1102mg sod., 9g carb. (4g sugars, 3g fiber), 14g pro.

MOROCCAN CAULIFLOWER & ALMOND SOUP

MOROCCAN CAULIFLOWER & ALMOND SOUP

This soup tastes rich and decadent but is really very healthy. Bonus—it is vegan and also makes your house smell amazing!
—*Barbara Marynowski, Hutto, TX*

PREP: 20 min. • **COOK:** 6 hours
MAKES: 8 servings

- 1   large head cauliflower (about 3½ lbs.), broken into florets
- 6   cups vegetable stock
- ¾   cup sliced almonds, toasted and divided
- ½   cup plus 2 Tbsp. minced fresh cilantro, divided
- 2   Tbsp. olive oil
- 1   to 3 tsp. harissa chili paste or hot pepper sauce
- ½   tsp. ground cinnamon
- ½   tsp. ground cumin
- ½   tsp. ground coriander
- 1¼ tsp. salt
- ½   tsp. pepper
      Additional harissa chili paste, optional

1. In a 5- or 6-qt. slow cooker, combine cauliflower, vegetable stock, ½ cup almonds, ½ cup cilantro and the next 7 ingredients. Cook, covered, on low until cauliflower is tender, 6-8 hours.
2. Puree soup using an immersion blender. Or cool slightly and puree soup in batches in a blender; return to slow cooker and heat through. Serve with remaining ¼ cup almonds and 2 Tbsp. cilantro and, if desired, additional harissa to taste.
Note: To toast nuts, bake in a shallow pan in a 350° oven (or cook in a skillet over low heat) until lightly browned, 5-10 minutes, stirring occasionally.
1¼ cups: 116 cal., 8g fat (1g sat. fat), 0 chol., 835mg sod., 9g carb. (2g sugars, 3g fiber), 4g pro.

TEST KITCHEN TIP
Harissa chili paste is a blend of different types of chiles, garlic, herbs and spices. Find it in jars in the spice section of your supermarket.

❄ ITALIAN VEGGIE BEEF SOUP

My sweet father-in-law, Pop Pop, would bring this chunky soup to our house when we were under the weather. We liked it so much that we now take it to our own friends who need comfort. Always does the trick.

—Sue Webb, Reisterstown, MD

- -

TAKES: 30 min. • **MAKES:** 12 servings (4 qt.)

- 1½ lbs. lean ground beef (90% lean)
- 2 medium onions, chopped
- 4 cups chopped cabbage
- 1 pkg. (16 oz.) frozen mixed vegetables
- 1 can (28 oz.) crushed tomatoes
- 1 bay leaf
- 3 tsp. Italian seasoning
- 1 tsp. salt
- ½ tsp. pepper
- 2 cartons (32 oz. each) reduced-sodium beef broth

1. In a 6-qt. stockpot, cook ground beef and onions over medium-high heat until beef is no longer pink, 6-8 minutes, breaking up beef into crumbles; drain.

2. Add cabbage, mixed vegetables, tomatoes, seasonings and broth; bring to a boil. Reduce heat; simmer, uncovered, until cabbage is crisp-tender, 10-15 minutes. Remove bay leaf.

Freeze option: Freeze cooled soup in freezer containers. To use, partially thaw overnight in refrigerator. Heat through in a saucepan, stirring occasionally; add broth if necessary.

1⅓ cups: 159 cal., 5g fat (2g sat. fat), 38mg chol., 646mg sod., 14g carb. (6g sugars, 4g fiber), 15g pro. **Diabetic exchanges:** 2 lean meat, 1 vegetable, ½ starch.

❄ 🍲 PIZZA SOUP WITH GARLIC TOAST CROUTONS

This comforting soup always satisfies my family's pizza cravings. I sometimes substitute Italian sausage for the chicken or add a little Parmesan cheese. Go nuts and add all your favorite pizza toppings!

—Joan Hallford, North Richland Hills, TX

- -

PREP: 10 min. • **COOK:** 6 hours
MAKES: 10 servings (about 4 qt.)

- 1 can (28 oz.) diced tomatoes, drained
- 1 can (15 oz.) pizza sauce
- 1 lb. boneless skinless chicken breasts, cut into 1-in. pieces
- 1 pkg. (3 oz.) sliced pepperoni, halved
- 1 cup sliced fresh mushrooms
- 1 small onion, chopped
- ½ cup chopped green pepper
- ¼ tsp. pepper
- 2 cans (14½ oz. each) chicken broth
- 1 pkg. (11¼ oz.) frozen garlic Texas toast
- 1 pkg. (10 oz.) frozen chopped spinach, thawed and squeezed dry
- 1 cup shredded part-skim mozzarella cheese

1. In a 6-qt. slow cooker, combine first 9 ingredients. Cook, covered, on low 6-8 hours, until chicken is tender.

2. For croutons, cut Texas toast into cubes; bake according to package directions. Add spinach to soup; heat through, stirring occasionally. Top servings with cheese and warm croutons.

Freeze option: Freeze cooled soup in freezer containers. To use, partially thaw overnight in refrigerator. Heat through in a saucepan, stirring occasionally. Prepare croutons as directed. Top soup with cheese and croutons.

1½ cups: 292 cal., 13g fat (5g sat. fat), 46mg chol., 1081mg sod., 24g carb. (7g sugars, 4g fiber), 20g pro.

TEST KITCHEN TIP
The garlic croutons and cheese put this soup over the top, but it's still amazing without them (and a lot leaner—just 150 calories and 6 grams of fat per serving).

PIZZA SOUP WITH GARLIC TOAST CROUTONS

EASY WHITE CHICKEN CHILI

Chili is one of our favorite cold-weather dishes. We like to use chicken and white beans for a twist on regular red chili. It's a truly soothing comfort food.
—*Rachel Lewis, Danville, VA*

TAKES: 30 min. • **MAKES:** 6 servings

- 1 lb. lean ground chicken
- 1 medium onion, chopped
- 2 cans (15 oz. each) cannellini beans, rinsed and drained
- 1 can (4 oz.) chopped green chiles
- 1 tsp. ground cumin
- ½ tsp. dried oregano
- ¼ tsp. pepper
- 1 can (14½ oz.) reduced-sodium chicken broth
   Optional toppings: Reduced-fat sour cream, shredded cheddar cheese and chopped fresh cilantro

1. In a large saucepan, cook chicken and onion over medium-high heat until chicken is no longer pink, 6-8 minutes, breaking up chicken into crumbles.
2. Pour 1 can of beans in a small bowl; mash slightly. Stir mashed beans, remaining can of beans, chiles, seasonings and broth into chicken mixture; bring to a boil. Reduce heat; simmer, covered, until flavors are blended, 12-15 minutes. Serve with toppings as desired.
Freeze option: Freeze cooled chili in freezer containers. To use, partially thaw overnight in refrigerator. Heat through in a saucepan, stirring occasionally; add broth if necessary.
1 cup: 228 cal., 5g fat (1g sat. fat), 54mg chol., 504mg sod., 23g carb. (1g sugars, 6g fiber), 22g pro. **Diabetic exchanges:** 3 lean meat, 1½ starch.

WHITE BEAN SOUP
WITH MEATBALLS

WHITE BEAN SOUP WITH MEATBALLS

It tastes like it's from scratch, but my Italian-inspired soup uses lots of shortcuts. For a meatball in every bite, chop them up—I like to use an egg slicer!
—*Carole Lotito, Hillsdale, NJ*

TAKES: 30 min. • **MAKES:** 6 servings

- 2 tsp. olive oil
- 1 medium onion, chopped
- 2 garlic cloves, minced
- ⅛ tsp. coarsely ground pepper
- 12 oz. frozen fully cooked Italian meatballs (about 3 cups), thawed
- 1 cup julienned carrots
- 1 carton (32 oz.) reduced-sodium chicken broth
- 1 can (15½ oz.) cannellini beans, rinsed and drained
- 8 cups coarsely chopped escarole (1 bunch) or fresh spinach
   Thinly sliced fresh basil, optional

1. In a 6-qt. stockpot, heat oil over medium heat; saute onion until tender, 3-4 minutes. Add garlic and pepper; cook and stir 1 minute.
2. Stir in the meatballs, carrots and broth; bring to a boil. Reduce heat; simmer, covered, 5 minutes. Stir in beans and escarole; return to a boil. Reduce heat; simmer, covered, until escarole has wilted, about 10 minutes. If desired, top servings with basil.
Freeze option: Freeze cooled soup in freezer containers. To use, partially thaw overnight in refrigerator. Heat through in a saucepan, stirring occasionally.
1 cup: 301 cal., 15g fat (6g sat. fat), 27mg chol., 1050mg sod., 26g carb. (3g sugars, 8g fiber), 19g pro.

READER REVIEW

"This soup is easy to make and absolutely delicious. I love all the distinct textures and flavors."

VIVIANBRADLEY, TASTEOFHOME.COM

FIRE-ROASTED TOMATO MINESTRONE

I created this recipe to accommodate my vegetarian guests at a Christmas dinner, but the soup was so delicious that we all enjoyed it! It can also be cooked on the stove for two hours on a low simmer.
—Donna-Marie Ryan, Topsfield, MA

- -

PREP: 20 min. • **COOK:** 4½ hours
MAKES: 8 servings (about 3 qt.)

- 1 medium sweet onion, chopped
- 1 cup cut fresh green beans
- 1 small zucchini, cubed
- 1 medium carrot, chopped
- 1 celery rib, chopped
- 2 garlic cloves, minced
- 2 Tbsp. olive oil
- ¼ tsp. salt
- ¼ tsp. pepper
- 2 cans (14½ oz. each) fire-roasted diced tomatoes
- 1 can (15 oz.) cannellini beans, rinsed and drained
- 1 carton (32 oz.) vegetable broth
- 1 cup uncooked small pasta shells
- 1 cup chopped fresh spinach
   Shredded Parmesan cheese, optional

1. In a 5-qt. slow cooker, combine the first 9 ingredients. Add tomatoes and beans; pour in broth. Cook, covered, on low until vegetables are tender, 4-6 hours.
2. Stir in pasta; cook, covered, on low until pasta is tender, 30-40 minutes. Stir in the spinach before serving. If desired, top with shredded Parmesan.
1⅓ cups: 175 cal., 4g fat (1g sat. fat), 0 chol., 767mg sod., 29g carb. (7g sugars, 5g fiber), 6g pro.

TEST KITCHEN TIP
To quickly peel fresh garlic, gently crush the clove with the flat side of a large knife blade to loosen the peel. If you don't have a large knife handy, you can crush the garlic with a small can.

FIRE-ROASTED TOMATO MINESTRONE

ROASTED CAULIFLOWER & RED PEPPER SOUP

ROASTED CAULIFLOWER & RED PEPPER SOUP

When cooler weather comes, soup is one of our favorite meals. I created this as a healthier version of all the cream-based soups out there. After a bit of trial and error, my husband and I decided this version is the keeper.
—*Elizabeth Bramkamp, Gig Harbor, WA*

- -

PREP: 50 min. + standing • **COOK:** 25 min.
MAKES: 6 servings

2	medium sweet red peppers, halved and seeded
1	large head cauliflower, broken into florets (about 7 cups)
4	Tbsp. olive oil, divided
1	cup chopped sweet onion
2	garlic cloves, minced
2½	tsp. minced fresh rosemary or ¾ tsp. dried rosemary, crushed
½	tsp. paprika
¼	cup all-purpose flour
4	cups chicken stock
1	cup 2% milk
½	tsp. salt
¼	tsp. pepper
⅛	to ¼ tsp. cayenne pepper
	Shredded Parmesan cheese, optional

1. Preheat broiler. Place the peppers on a foil-lined baking sheet, skin side up. Broil 4 in. from heat until the skins are blistered, about 5 minutes. Transfer to a bowl; let stand, covered, 20 minutes. Change oven setting to bake; preheat oven to 400°.

2. Toss cauliflower with 2 Tbsp. oil; spread in a 15x10x1-in. pan. Roast until tender, 25-30 minutes, stirring occasionally. Remove skin and seeds from peppers; chop peppers.

3. In a 6-qt. stockpot, heat remaining 2 Tbsp. oil over medium heat. Add onion; cook until golden and softened, 6-8 minutes, stirring occasionally. Add the garlic, rosemary and paprika; cook and stir 1 minute. Stir in flour until blended; cook and stir 1 minute. Gradually stir in stock. Bring to a boil, stirring constantly; cook and stir until thickened.

4. Stir in cauliflower and peppers. Puree soup using an immersion blender. Or, cool slightly and puree soup in batches in a blender; return to pot. Stir in milk and remaining seasonings; heat through. If desired, serve with Parmesan.

Freeze option: Freeze the cooled soup in freezer containers. To use, partially thaw overnight in refrigerator. Heat through in a saucepan, stirring occasionally; add stock or milk if necessary.

1 cup: 193 cal., 10g fat (2g sat. fat), 3mg chol., 601mg sod., 19g carb. (8g sugars, 4g fiber), 8g pro. **Diabetic exchanges:** 2 vegetable, 2 fat, ½ starch.

PESTO BEAN SOUP

This is one of my favorite vegetarian recipes, especially on cold winter evenings. I make large batches and freeze it. Homemade pesto is tasty, but you can use store-bought to make the recipe really simple. Serve the soup with garlic toast and a green salad.
—*Liz Bellville, Tonasket, WA*

PREP: 10 min. • **COOK:** 4 hours
MAKES: 8 servings (2½ qt.)

- 1   carton (32 oz.) reduced-sodium vegetable broth
- 1   large white onion, chopped
- 4   garlic cloves, minced
- 2½ cups sliced baby portobello mushrooms
- 3   cans (15 oz. each) cannellini beans, rinsed and drained
- ¾   cup prepared pesto, divided
- ¼   cup grated Parmigiano-Reggiano cheese
      Optional: Additional pesto and cheese

In a 4-qt. slow cooker, combine the first 5 ingredients. Stir in ½ cup pesto. Cook, covered, on low until vegetables are tender, 4-6 hours. Before serving, stir in remaining ¼ cup pesto and the cheese. If desired, serve with additional pesto and cheese.

1¼ cups: 244 cal., 9g fat (2g sat. fat), 2mg chol., 586mg sod., 30g carb. (3g sugars, 8g fiber), 9g pro. **Diabetic exchanges:** 2 starch, 1½ fat, 1 lean meat.

SWEET-AND-SOUR BEEF STEW

SWEET-AND-SOUR BEEF STEW

This chunky meal in a bowl has a deliciously sweet and tangy taste. And it makes terrific use of nutrient-packed vegetables.
—*Frances Conklin, Cottonwood, ID*

PREP: 25 min. • **COOK:** 8 hours
MAKES: 8 servings (2 quarts)

- 2   lbs. beef top round steak, cut into 1-in. cubes
- 2   Tbsp. olive oil
- 1   can (15 oz.) tomato sauce
- 2   large onions, chopped
- 4   medium carrots, thinly sliced
- 1   large green pepper, cut into 1-in. pieces
- 1   cup canned pineapple chunks, drained
- ½   cup cider vinegar
- ¼   cup packed brown sugar
- ¼   cup light corn syrup
- 2   tsp. chili powder
- 2   tsp. paprika
- ½   tsp. salt
      Hot cooked rice, optional

1. In a large skillet, brown beef in oil in batches; drain. Transfer to a 4- or 5-qt. slow cooker.
2. In a large bowl, combine the tomato sauce, onions, carrots, green pepper, pineapple, vinegar, brown sugar, corn syrup, chili powder, paprika and salt; pour over beef.
3. Cover and cook on low for 8-10 hours or until beef is tender. Serve with rice if desired.

Freeze option: Freeze cooled stew in freezer containers. To use, partially thaw overnight in refrigerator. Heat through in a saucepan, stirring occasionally; add broth or water if necessary.

1 cup: 290 cal., 7g fat (2g sat. fat), 64mg chol., 465mg sod., 29g carb. (17g sugars, 3g fiber), 28g pro. **Diabetic exchanges:** 3 lean meat, 2 vegetable, 1 starch, ½ fat.

READER REVIEW

"Loved this! So good. Will make again with pork or maybe chicken. This is a keeper."

HEART4ASIA, TASTEOFHOME.COM

TOMATO BASIL TORTELLINI SOUP

When my family tried this soup, they all had to have seconds, and my husband is happy any time I put it on the table. Sometimes I add cooked, crumbled bacon and serve the soup topped with mozzarella cheese.
—*Christina Addison, Blanchester, OH*

PREP: 25 min. • **COOK:** 6¼ hours
MAKES: 18 servings (4½ qt.)

- 2 Tbsp. olive oil
- 1 medium onion, chopped
- 3 medium carrots, chopped
- 5 garlic cloves, minced
- 3 cans (28 oz. each) crushed tomatoes, undrained
- 1 carton (32 oz.) vegetable broth
- 1 Tbsp. sugar
- 1 tsp. dried basil
- 1 bay leaf
- 3 pkg. (9 oz. each) refrigerated cheese tortellini
- ¾ cup half-and-half cream
  Shredded Parmesan cheese and minced fresh basil

1. In a large skillet, heat oil over medium-high heat. Add onion and carrots; cook and stir until crisp-tender, 5-6 minutes. Add garlic; cook 1 minute longer. Transfer to a 6- or 7-qt. slow cooker. Add the tomatoes, broth, sugar, basil and bay leaf. Cook, covered, on low until vegetables are tender, 6-7 hours.
2. Stir in tortellini. Cook, covered, on high 15 minutes. Reduce heat to low; stir in cream until heated through. Discard bay leaf. Serve topped with Parmesan cheese and basil.
Freeze option: Before stirring in half-and-half, cool soup and freeze in freezer containers. To use, partially thaw in refrigerator overnight. Heat through in a saucepan, stirring occasionally; add half-and-half as directed.
1 cup: 214 cal., 7g fat (3g sat. fat), 23mg chol., 569mg sod., 32g carb. (9g sugars, 4g fiber), 9g pro. **Diabetic exchanges:** 2 starch, 1 fat.

TEST KITCHEN TIP
If you're cooking for a smaller group, make just one-third of the recipe in a small slow cooker and decrease the cooking time slightly.

NO-FUSS POTATO SOUP

For a busy-day supper, my family loves to have big steaming bowls of this delicious soup, along with fresh bread from our bread machine.
—*Dotty Egge, Pelican Rapids, MN*

PREP: 15 min. • **COOK:** 7½ hours
MAKES: 10 servings (about 2½ qt.)

- 6 cups cubed peeled potatoes
- 5 cups water
- 2 cups chopped onions
- ½ cup chopped celery
- ½ cup thinly sliced carrots
- ¼ cup butter, cubed
- 4 tsp. chicken bouillon granules or 2 vegetable bouillon cubes
- 2 tsp. salt
- ¼ tsp. pepper
- 1 can (12 oz.) evaporated milk
- 3 Tbsp. minced fresh parsley
  Minced chives, optional

1. In a 5-qt. slow cooker, combine the first 9 ingredients. Cover and cook on low for 7-8 hours or until the vegetables are tender.
2. Add milk and parsley. Cover and cook 30 minutes longer or until heated through. Garnish with chives if desired.
1 cup: 190 cal., 7g fat (0 sat. fat), 12mg chol., 827mg sod., 26g carb. (0 sugars, 0 fiber), 5g pro. **Diabetic exchanges:** 1½ starch, 1½ fat, 1 vegetable.

TOMATO BASIL TORTELLINI SOUP

TACO-FILLED
PASTA SHELLS, P. 49

Beef Entrees

Meat lovers, rejoice! This chapter shows you how a bit of planning leads to hearty dinners even on busy days.

SOUTHWESTERN CASSEROLE, P. 44

COFFEE-BRAISED ROAST BEEF

This recipe has been a family tradition since 1974. It makes a quick and tasty meal that is a nice welcome home after a long day of work. The coffee adds an intriguing flavor to the roast, and the juices can be thickened for a delicious gravy.
—*Nancy Schuler, Belle Fourche, SD*

PREP: 10 min. + marinating
COOK: 6½ hours
MAKES: 10 servings

- 1 cup cider vinegar
- 4 garlic cloves, crushed, divided
- 1 boneless beef chuck roast (4 to 5 lbs.), trimmed
- 2 tsp. salt
- 1 tsp. pepper
- 1 cup strong brewed coffee
- 1 cup beef broth
- 1 medium onion, sliced
- 3 Tbsp. cornstarch
- ¼ cup cold water
  Mashed potatoes

1. In a large shallow dish, combine vinegar and 2 garlic cloves. Add roast; turn to coat. Cover and refrigerate overnight, turning occasionally.
2. Drain roast, discarding marinade. Pat roast dry; sprinkle with salt and pepper. Place roast in a 5- or 6-qt. slow cooker; add coffee, broth, onion and the remaining 2 cloves garlic. Cook, covered, on low until meat is tender, 6-7 hours.
3. Remove roast and keep warm. Strain cooking juices, discarding onion and garlic; skim fat. In a small bowl, mix cornstarch and cold water until smooth; gradually stir into slow cooker. Cook, covered, on high until gravy is thickened, about 30 minutes. Slice roast; serve with mashed potatoes and gravy.
5 oz. cooked beef with ½ cup gravy: 324 cal., 17g fat (7g sat. fat), 118mg chol., 636mg sod., 3g carb. (0 sugars, 0 fiber), 36g pro.

BALSAMIC BEEF HOAGIES

All my boys (big and small) like sandwiches, and balsamic beef is a welcome change from pulled barbecued chicken. We use leftovers in quesadillas, on pizza or with rice. You can find more family-friendly recipes at my blog, theseasonedmom.com.
—*Blair Lonergan, Rochelle, VA*

PREP: 25 min. • **COOK:** 5 hours
MAKES: 8 servings

- 1 cup beef broth
- ½ cup balsamic vinegar
- 2 Tbsp. brown sugar
- 2 Tbsp. Worcestershire sauce
- 4 garlic cloves, minced
- 1 boneless beef chuck roast (2 lbs.)

SANDWICHES
- ½ cup mayonnaise
- 8 hoagie buns, split and toasted
- 4 medium tomatoes, sliced
- ½ cup thinly sliced fresh basil

1. In a small bowl, mix the first 5 ingredients. Place roast in a 4- or 5-qt. slow cooker. Pour broth mixture over top. Cook, covered, on low until meat is tender, 5-6 hours.
2. Remove roast; shred beef with 2 forks. Skim fat from cooking juices. Return beef and cooking juices to slow cooker; heat through.
3. Spread mayonnaise on buns. Using tongs, place the beef on buns; top with tomatoes and basil.
Freeze option: Freeze cooled meat mixture in freezer containers. To use, partially thaw in refrigerator overnight. Heat through in a saucepan, stirring occasionally; add broth if necessary.
1 sandwich: 549 cal., 26g fat (7g sat. fat), 79mg chol., 669mg sod., 46g carb. (14g sugars, 2g fiber), 31g pro.

COFFEE-BRAISED ROAST BEEF

PIZZA NOODLE BAKE

BEEF KABOBS WITH CHUTNEY SAUCE

I created this speedy grilled entree for our daughter, who is a fan of Indian food. The mango chutney and touch of curry give the beef a sweet and spicy flavor.
—Judy Thompson, Ankeny, IA

PREP: 15 min. + marinating • **GRILL:** 5 min.
MAKES: 8 kabobs (about ½ cup sauce)

- ¼ cup mango chutney
- 1 Tbsp. water
- 1 Tbsp. cider vinegar
- 1 tsp. curry powder
- ¼ tsp. cayenne pepper
- 1 lb. beef top sirloin steak, cut into ¼-in. strips

CHUTNEY SAUCE
- ½ cup plain yogurt
- 3 Tbsp. mango chutney
- 1 tsp. lemon juice
- ½ tsp. curry powder
- ¼ tsp. ground cumin
- ⅛ tsp. cayenne pepper

1. In a large shallow dish, combine the first 5 ingredients. Add the beef; turn to coat. Refrigerate, covered, overnight.
2. In a small bowl, combine sauce ingredients. Cover and refrigerate until serving.
3. Drain beef, discarding marinade. Thread beef onto 8 metal or soaked wooden skewers.
4. On a lightly oiled grill rack, grill the kabobs, covered, over medium heat (or broil 4 in. from heat) 4-6 minutes or until the meat reaches desired doneness, turning occasionally. Serve with sauce.

2 skewers with 2 Tbsp. sauce: 258 cal., 6g fat (2g sat. fat), 50mg chol., 321mg sod., 23g carb. (15g sugars, 0 fiber), 25g pro. **Diabetic exchanges:** 3 lean meat, 1½ starch.

DID YOU KNOW?
Mango chutney is a jam-like sauce that's flavored with mild spices and made without additional pectin. Look for it in the Indian-foods aisle at the grocery store or with the jams and jellies. In a pinch, you can replace mango chutney with apricot preserves.

❄ PIZZA NOODLE BAKE

Here's a family-pleasing casserole that comes together in a snap. It's perfect for a weeknight meal. I like to double the recipe and freeze one for later!
—Bernice Knutson, Soldier, IA

PREP: 25 min. • **BAKE:** 15 min.
MAKES: 6 servings

- 10 oz. uncooked egg noodles
- 1½ lbs. ground beef
- ½ cup finely chopped onion
- ¼ cup chopped green pepper
- 1 jar (14 oz.) pizza sauce
- 1 can (4 oz.) mushroom stems and pieces, drained
- 1 cup shredded cheddar cheese
- 1 cup shredded part-skim mozzarella cheese
- 1 pkg. (3½ oz.) sliced pepperoni

1. Cook noodles according to the package directions. Meanwhile, in a large skillet, cook beef, onion and green pepper over medium heat until beef is no longer pink, breaking beef into crumbles; drain. Add pizza sauce and mushrooms; heat through.
2. Drain the noodles. In a greased 13x9-in. baking dish, layer half the noodles, half the beef mixture, ½ cup of each cheese and half the pepperoni. Repeat the layers. Cover and bake casserole at 350° for 15-20 minutes or until heated through.
Freeze option: Cover and freeze unbaked casserole for up to 3 months. Remove from the freezer 30 minutes before baking (do not thaw). Cover; bake at 350° for 45-50 minutes. Uncover; bake 15-20 minutes longer or until heated through.

1⅓ cups: 644 cal., 33g fat (15g sat. fat), 160mg chol., 913mg sod., 42g carb. (6g sugars, 4g fiber), 43g pro.

INDIVIDUAL
SHEPHERD'S PIES

❄

INDIVIDUAL
SHEPHERD'S PIES

These comforting little pies make a fun St. Patrick's Day surprise for the family. Extras are easy to freeze for busy weeknights.
—*Ellen Osborne, Clarksville, TN*

PREP: 30 min. • **BAKE:** 20 min.
MAKES: 10 mini pies

1	lb. ground beef
3	Tbsp. chopped onion
½	tsp. minced garlic
⅓	cup chili sauce or ketchup
1	Tbsp. cider vinegar
2	cups hot mashed potatoes (with added 2% milk and butter)
3	oz. cream cheese, softened
1	tube (12 oz.) refrigerated buttermilk biscuits
½	cup crushed potato chips
	Paprika, optional

1. Preheat oven to 375°. In a large skillet, cook beef and onion over medium heat until beef is no longer pink, 5-7 minutes, breaking up beef into crumbles. Add garlic; cook 1 minute or until tender. Drain. Stir in the chili sauce and cider vinegar.
2. In a small bowl, mix mashed potatoes and cream cheese until blended. Press 1 biscuit onto the bottom and up the sides of each of 10 greased muffin cups. Fill with beef mixture. Spread potato mixture over tops. Sprinkle with potato chips, pressing down lightly.
3. Bake until golden brown, 20-25 minutes. If desired, sprinkle with paprika.
Freeze option: Freeze cooled shepherd's pies in a single layer in freezer containers. To use, partially thaw in refrigerator overnight. Bake on a baking sheet in a preheated 375° oven until heated through, 15-18 minutes.
2 mini pies: 567 cal., 30g fat (12g sat. fat), 84mg chol., 1378mg sod., 51g carb. (9g sugars, 2g fiber), 23g pro.

MAKE-AHEAD SPICY
OLIVE PASTA

TANGY BARBECUE SANDWICHES

Because I prepare the beef for these robust sandwiches in the slow cooker, it's easy to fix a meal for a hungry bunch. The savory homemade sauce assures that I come home with no leftovers.

—Debbi Smith, Crossett, AR

PREP: 10 min. • **COOK:** 7½ hours
MAKES: 18 sandwiches

- 3 cups chopped celery
- 1 cup chopped onion
- 1 cup ketchup
- 1 cup barbecue sauce
- 1 cup water
- 2 Tbsp. white vinegar
- 2 Tbsp. Worcestershire sauce
- 2 Tbsp. brown sugar
- 1 tsp. chili powder
- 1 tsp. salt
- ½ tsp. pepper
- ½ tsp. garlic powder
- 1 boneless beef chuck roast (3 to 4 lbs.), trimmed and cut in half
- 18 hamburger buns, split

1. In a 5-qt. slow cooker, combine the first 12 ingredients. Add roast. Cover and cook on high for 1 hour. Reduce heat to low and cook 6-8 hours longer or until meat is tender.

2. Remove roast; cool. Shred meat and return to sauce; heat through. Using a slotted spoon, fill each bun with about ½ cup of meat mixture.

1 sandwich: 262 cal., 9g fat (3g sat. fat), 49mg chol., 659mg sod., 26g carb. (8g sugars, 2g fiber), 18g pro.

SOUTHWESTERN CASSEROLE

SOUTHWESTERN CASSEROLE

I've been making this family-pleasing dish for years. It tastes wonderful, fits nicely into our budget and, best of all, makes a second casserole to freeze and enjoy later.

—Joan Hallford, North Richland Hills, TX

PREP: 25 min. • **BAKE:** 40 min.
MAKES: 2 casseroles (6 servings each)

- 2 cups (8 oz.) uncooked elbow macaroni
- 2 lbs. ground beef
- 1 large onion, chopped
- 2 garlic cloves, minced
- 2 cans (14½ oz. each) diced tomatoes, undrained
- 1 can (16 oz.) kidney beans, rinsed and drained
- 1 can (6 oz.) tomato paste
- 1 can (4 oz.) chopped green chiles, drained
- 1½ tsp. salt
- 1 tsp. chili powder
- ½ tsp. ground cumin
- ½ tsp. pepper
- 2 cups shredded Monterey Jack cheese
- 2 jalapeno peppers, seeded and chopped

1. Cook macaroni according to package directions. Meanwhile, in a large saucepan, cook beef and onion over medium heat, crumbling beef, until beef is no longer pink. Add garlic; cook 1 minute longer. Drain. Stir in next 8 ingredients. Bring to a boil. Reduce heat; simmer, uncovered, 10 minutes. Drain macaroni; stir into beef mixture.

2. Preheat oven to 375°. Transfer macaroni mixture to 2 greased 2-qt. baking dishes. Top with cheese and jalapenos. Cover and bake at 375° for 30 minutes. Uncover; bake until bubbly and heated through, about 10 minutes longer. Serve 1 casserole. Cool the second; cover and freeze up to 3 months.

To use frozen casserole: Thaw in refrigerator 8 hours. Preheat oven to 375°. Remove from refrigerator 30 minutes before baking. Cover and bake, increasing time as necessary to heat through and for a thermometer inserted in center to read 165°, 20-25 minutes.

Note: Wear disposable gloves when cutting hot peppers; the oils can burn skin. Avoid touching your face.

1 cup: 321 cal., 15g fat (7g sat. fat), 64mg chol., 673mg sod., 23g carb. (5g sugars, 4g fiber), 24g pro.

BEEF CHIMICHANGAS

My husband loves these beef chimichangas! I double the recipe and freeze the chimichangas individually to take out as needed. I serve them with shredded lettuce and sour cream.
—*Schelby Thompson, Camden Wyoming, DE*

PREP: 25 min. • **COOK:** 15 min.
MAKES: 1 dozen

- 1 lb. ground beef
- 1 can (16 oz.) refried beans
- ½ cup finely chopped onion
- 3 cans (8 oz. each) tomato sauce, divided
- 2 tsp. chili powder
- 1 tsp. minced garlic
- ½ tsp. ground cumin
- 12 flour tortillas (10 in.), warmed
- 1 can (4 oz.) chopped green chiles
- 1 can (4 oz.) chopped jalapeno peppers
  Oil for deep-fat frying
- 1½ cups shredded cheddar cheese

1. In a large skillet, cook beef over medium heat, crumbling beef, until no longer pink; drain. Stir in the beans, onion, ½ cup tomato sauce, chili powder, garlic and cumin.
2. Spoon about ⅓ cup of mixture off-center on each tortilla. Fold edge nearest filling up and over to cover. Fold in both sides and roll up. Fasten with toothpicks. In a large saucepan, combine the chiles, peppers and remaining tomato sauce; heat through.
3. In an electric skillet or deep-fat fryer, heat 1 in. of oil to 375°. Fry the chimichangas for 1½-2 minutes on each side or until browned. Drain on paper towels. Sprinkle with cheese. Serve with sauce.

1 chimichanga: 626 cal., 41g fat (9g sat. fat), 37mg chol., 1094mg sod., 46g carb. (5g sugars, 6g fiber), 19g pro.

> **DID YOU KNOW?**
> You can bake chimichangas instead of frying them. Brush with melted butter and bake at 350° until golden brown, 25-30 minutes. (If frozen, thaw before baking.)

❄

BEEF TACO LASAGNA

This recipe makes two big pans. Freeze one or both to enjoy later.
—*Stacey Compton, Toledo, OH*

PREP: 30 min. • **BAKE:** 35 min. + standing
MAKES: 2 casseroles (8 pieces each)

- 24 lasagna noodles
- 2 lbs. lean ground beef (90% lean)
- 2 envelopes taco seasoning
- 4 large egg whites
- 2 cartons (15 oz. each) ricotta cheese
- 8 cups shredded cheddar cheese
- 2 jars (24 oz. each) chunky salsa

1. Preheat oven to 350°. Cook the noodles according to package directions. Meanwhile, in a large skillet, cook beef over medium heat, crumbling beef, until no longer pink; drain. Stir in taco seasoning. In a small bowl, combine egg whites and ricotta cheese. Drain noodles.
2. In each of two 13x9-in. baking dishes, layer 4 noodles, ⅔ cup ricotta mixture, half the beef mixture and 1⅓ cups cheddar cheese. Top each with 4 noodles, ⅔ cup ricotta mixture, 1⅓ cups salsa and 1⅓ cups cheese. For final layer, top each with 4 noodles, ⅔ cup ricotta mixture, 1⅓ cups salsa and 1⅓ cups cheese.
3. Bake, uncovered, 35-40 minutes or until heated through. Let stand for 10 minutes before cutting.

Freeze option: Cover and freeze unbaked lasagna. To use, partially thaw overnight in refrigerator. Remove from refrigerator 30 minutes before baking. Bake as directed, increasing time if needed to heat through until a thermometer inserted in center reads 165°.

1 piece: 545 cal., 26g fat (17g sat. fat), 109mg chol., 1198mg sod., 42g carb. (7g sugars, 1g fiber), 35g pro.

BEEF CHIMICHANGAS

DEBRA'S CAVATINI

❄ DEBRA'S CAVATINI

I love this recipe because it makes two hearty casseroles. I add a little something different every time I make it, such as extra garlic, to give it an added boost of flavor.
—*Debra Butcher, Decatur, IN*

- -

PREP: 45 min. • **BAKE:** 35 min.
MAKES: 2 casseroles (6 servings each)

- 1   pkg. (16 oz.) penne pasta
- 1   lb. ground beef
- 1   lb. bulk Italian pork sausage
- 1¾ cups sliced fresh mushrooms
- 1   medium onion, chopped
- 1   medium green pepper, chopped
- 2   cans (14½ oz. each) Italian diced tomatoes
- 1   jar (23½ oz.) Italian sausage and garlic spaghetti sauce
- 1   jar (16 oz.) chunky mild salsa
- 1   pkg. (8 oz.) sliced pepperoni, chopped
- 1   cup shredded Swiss cheese, divided
- 4   cups shredded part-skim mozzarella cheese, divided
- 1½ cups shredded Parmesan cheese, divided
- 1   jar (24 oz.) 3-cheese spaghetti sauce

1. Cook the pasta according to the package directions. Meanwhile, in a Dutch oven, cook beef, sausage, mushrooms, onion and green pepper over medium heat until beef is no longer pink, breaking beef into crumbles; drain.

2. Drain the pasta; add to the meat mixture. Stir in the tomatoes, spaghetti sauce, salsa and pepperoni.

3. Preheat oven to 350°. Divide half the pasta mixture between 2 greased 13x9-in. baking dishes. Sprinkle each with ¼ cup Swiss cheese, 1 cup mozzarella cheese and ⅓ cup Parmesan cheese. Spread ¾ cup 3-cheese spaghetti sauce over each. Top with remaining pasta mixture and 3-cheese spaghetti sauce. Sprinkle with remaining cheeses.

4. Cover and bake until bubbly, 25 minutes. Uncover; bake until cheese is melted, about 10 minutes longer.

Freeze option: Cover unbaked casserole and freeze for up to 3 months. To use, thaw casserole in refrigerator overnight. Remove from refrigerator 30 minutes before baking. Preheat oven to 350°. Bake casserole, covered, 45 minutes. Uncover; bake about 10 minutes or until cheese is melted.

1½ cups: 708 cal., 38g fat (16g sat. fat), 106mg chol., 1788mg sod., 54g carb. (18g sugars, 5g fiber), 38g pro.

SLOW-COOKER
BEEF BARBACOA

SLOW-COOKER BEEF BARBACOA

I love this beef barbacoa because the meat is fall-apart tender and the sauce is smoky, slightly spicy and so flavorful. It's an amazing alternative to ground beef or pulled pork carnitas. It's also versatile. You can have a taco bar and let people make their own tacos—or create mouthwatering rice bowls or even Mexican pizzas.
—*Holly Sander, Lake Mary, FL*

PREP: 20 min. • **COOK:** 6 hours
MAKES: 8 servings

  1 beef rump or bottom
     round roast (3 lbs.)
  ½ cup minced fresh cilantro
  ⅓ cup tomato paste
  8 garlic cloves, minced
  2 Tbsp. chipotle peppers in
     adobo sauce plus 1 Tbsp. adobo sauce
  2 Tbsp. cider vinegar
  4 tsp. ground cumin
  1 Tbsp. brown sugar
  1½ tsp. salt
  1 tsp. pepper
  1 cup beef stock
  1 cup beer or additional beef stock
  16 corn tortillas (6 in.)
     Pico de gallo
     Optional toppings: Lime wedges,
     queso fresco and additional cilantro

1. Cut roast in half. Mix next 9 ingredients; rub over roast. Place in a 5-qt. slow cooker. Add stock and beer. Cook, covered, until meat is tender, 6-8 hours.
2. Remove roast; shred with 2 forks. Reserve 3 cups cooking juices; discard remaining juices. Skim fat from reserved juices. Return beef and reserved juices to slow cooker; heat through.
3. Serve with corn tortillas and pico de gallo. If desired, serve with lime wedges, queso fresco and additional cilantro.
Freeze option: Place shredded beef in freezer containers. Cool and freeze. To use, partially thaw in refrigerator overnight. Heat through in a covered saucepan, stirring gently; add broth if necessary.
2 filled tortillas: 361 cal., 10g fat (3g sat. fat), 101mg chol., 652mg sod., 28g carb. (4g sugars, 4g fiber), 38g pro. **Diabetic exchanges:** 5 lean meat, 2 starch.

OVEN-BAKED BRISKET

Texans like brisket cooked on the smoker, but this recipe offers convenient prep in the oven. I make extra sauce to serve on the side. Round out the meal with potato salad and slaw.
—*Katie Ferrier, Houston, TX*

PREP: 15 min. + marinating • **BAKE:** 4¼ hours
MAKES: 8 servings

- 1 fresh beef brisket (4 to 5 lbs.)
- 2 Tbsp. Worcestershire sauce
- 2 Tbsp. soy sauce
- 1 Tbsp. onion salt
- 1 Tbsp. liquid smoke
- 2 tsp. salt
- 2 tsp. pepper
  Dash hot pepper sauce

SAUCE

- ½ cup ketchup
- 3 Tbsp. brown sugar
- 1 Tbsp. lemon juice
- 1 Tbsp. soy sauce
- 1 tsp. ground mustard
- 3 drops hot pepper sauce
  Dash ground nutmeg

1. Place brisket, fat side down, in a 13x9-in. baking dish. In a bowl, mix Worcestershire sauce, soy sauce, onion salt, liquid smoke, salt, pepper and hot pepper sauce; pour over brisket. Turn brisket fat side up; refrigerate, covered, overnight.

2. Remove brisket from refrigerator. Preheat oven to 300°. Bake, covered, 4 hours. In a small bowl, combine sauce ingredients. Spread over brisket. Bake, uncovered, 15-30 minutes longer or until tender. Cut diagonally across the grain into thin slices.

6 oz. cooked beef: 334 cal., 10g fat (4g sat. fat), 97mg chol., 1922mg sod., 11g carb. (10g sugars, 0 fiber), 48g pro.

Note: This recipe calls for a fresh beef brisket, not corned beef.

❄

SMOKY BRAISED CHUCK ROAST

After tiring of the same sauces, I began experimenting with spices and flavors, and came up with this concoction. It's excellent with steak, London broil or a roast, and delivers the flavor of a summer cookout all year long!
—*Karen Brown, Tunkhannock, PA*

PREP: 15 min. + marinating • **BAKE:** 2½ hours
MAKES: 8 servings

- 4 tsp. beef bouillon granules
- ¼ cup hot water
- 1¾ cups water
- 2 Tbsp. brown sugar
- 1 tsp. dried rosemary, crushed
- 1 tsp. dried basil
- ¾ tsp. dried tarragon
- ½ tsp. garlic powder
- ¼ tsp. dried oregano
  Dash pepper
- ½ tsp. liquid smoke, optional
- 1 beef chuck roast (3 to 4 lbs.)

1. In a 13x9-in. baking dish, dissolve bouillon in hot water. Stir in the water, brown sugar, seasonings and, if desired, liquid smoke. Add chuck roast; turn to coat. Cover and refrigerate overnight.

2. Preheat oven to 325°. Transfer roast to a Dutch oven; pour remaining marinade over top. Bake, covered, until tender, 2½-3 hours.

Freeze option: Place sliced chuck roast in freezer containers; top with cooking juices. Cool and freeze. To use, partially thaw in refrigerator overnight. Microwave, covered, on high, stirring gently until heated through; add broth if necessary, .

4 oz. cooked beef: 305 cal., 16g fat (6g sat. fat), 111mg chol., 465mg sod., 4g carb. (4g sugars, 0 fiber), 34g pro.

OVEN-BAKED BRISKET

**TACO-FILLED
PASTA SHELLS**

MEATBALLS IN HONEY BUFFALO SAUCE

My family loves sweet and spicy combinations and declared this recipe an instant favorite just for that reason. The meatballs start sweet but finish with a little heat!
—*Anne Ormond, Dover, NH*

- -

PREP: 45 min. • **COOK:** 2 hours
MAKES: about 2½ dozen

- 2 large eggs, lightly beaten
- 15 Ritz crackers, crushed
- ½ medium onion, finely chopped
- ¼ cup 2% milk
- 4 tsp. brown sugar
- ½ tsp. garlic powder
- ½ tsp. ground chipotle pepper
- ¼ tsp. smoked paprika
- ¼ tsp. salt
- ⅛ tsp. pepper
- ½ lb. ground beef
- ½ lb. ground pork
- ½ lb. ground veal

SAUCE
- ½ cup honey
- ¼ cup Buffalo wing sauce
- ¼ cup packed brown sugar
- 2 Tbsp. orange marmalade
- 2 Tbsp. apricot spreadable fruit
- 2 Tbsp. reduced-sodium soy sauce
- ¼ tsp. crushed red pepper flakes
  Hot cooked rice or pasta
  Sliced celery, optional

1. Preheat oven to 400°. Combine first 10 ingredients. Add meat; mix lightly but thoroughly. Shape meat mixture into 1½-in. balls; bake on a greased rack in a 15x10x1-in. baking pan lined with foil until lightly browned, 12-15 minutes. Meanwhile, in a small saucepan over medium heat, whisk together sauce ingredients until brown sugar is dissolved.
2. Transfer meatballs to a 3-qt. slow cooker; add sauce. Cook, covered, on low until the meatballs are cooked through, about 2 hours. Serve with hot cooked rice or pasta and, if desired, sliced celery.

Freeze option: Freeze cooled meatballs and sauce in freezer containers. To use, partially thaw in refrigerator overnight. Heat through in a covered saucepan, stirring gently; add water or broth if necessary. Serve as directed.

3 meatballs with 2 Tbsp. sauce: 258 cal., 10g fat (3g sat. fat), 81mg chol., 459mg sod., 30g carb. (26g sugars, 0 fiber), 14g pro.

TACO-FILLED PASTA SHELLS

I've been stuffing pasta shells with different fillings for years, but my family enjoys this version with taco-seasoned meat the most. The frozen shells are so convenient, because you can take out only the number you need for a single-serving lunch or family dinner. Just add zippy taco sauce and bake.
—*Marge Hodel, Roanoke, IL*

- -

PREP: 20 min. + chilling • **BAKE:** 45 min.
MAKES: 2 casseroles (6 servings each)

- 2 lbs. ground beef
- 2 envelopes taco seasoning
- 1½ cups water
- 1 pkg. (8 oz.) cream cheese, cubed
- 24 uncooked jumbo pasta shells
- ¼ cup butter, melted

ADDITIONAL INGREDIENTS
  (FOR EACH CASSEROLE)
- 1 cup salsa
- 1 cup taco sauce
- 1 cup shredded cheddar cheese
- 1 cup shredded Monterey Jack cheese
- 1½ cups crushed tortilla chips
- 1 cup sour cream
- 3 green onions, chopped

1. In a Dutch oven, cook beef over medium heat, crumbling beef, until no longer pink; drain. Stir in taco seasoning and water. Bring to a boil. Reduce heat; simmer, uncovered, for 5 minutes. Stir in cream cheese until melted. Transfer to a bowl; cool. Chill for 1 hour.
2. Cook pasta according to package directions; drain. Gently toss with butter. Fill each shell with about 3 Tbsp. of meat mixture. Place 12 filled shells in a freezer container. Cover and freeze for up to 3 months.
3. To prepare remaining 12 filled shells, spoon 1 cup salsa into a greased 9-in. square baking dish. Top with shells and 1 cup taco sauce. Cover and bake at 350° for 30 minutes. Uncover; sprinkle with 1 cup of each cheese and 1½ cups chips. Bake 15 minutes longer or until heated through. Serve with sour cream and onions.

Freeze option: To use frozen shells, thaw in the refrigerator for 24 hours (shells will be partially frozen). Spoon 1 cup salsa into a greased 9-in. square baking dish; top with shells and 1 cup taco sauce. Cover and bake at 350° for 40 minutes. Uncover. Sprinkle with 1 cup of each cheese and 1½ cups chips. Bake 15 minutes longer or until heated through. Serve with sour cream and onions.

2 shells: 492 cal., 31g fat (16g sat. fat), 98mg chol., 982mg sod., 29g carb. (4g sugars, 1g fiber), 23g pro.

SAUCY INDIAN-STYLE
CHICKEN & VEGETABLES, P. 55

Chicken & Turkey Suppers

These easy down-home favorites are the dishes to keep in your regular rotation.

CRANBERRY CHIPOTLE
CHICKEN ENCHILADAS, P. 59

CHICKEN PIZZA

This fun twist on typical pizza is an excellent way to use up leftover pesto. And since it's loaded with protein-rich chicken and black beans, it's hearty enough to satisfy everyone.
—Taste of Home *Test Kitchen*

TAKES: 30 min. • **MAKES:** 6 pieces

- 1 lb. boneless skinless chicken breasts, cut into 1-in. pieces
- 1 Tbsp. olive oil
- 1 prebaked 12-in. pizza crust
- ¼ cup prepared pesto
- 1 large tomato, chopped
- ½ cup canned black beans, rinsed and drained
- 1 cup shredded part-skim mozzarella cheese
- ½ cup shredded Parmesan cheese

1. In a large skillet, cook and stir chicken in oil over medium heat 10-15 minutes or until no longer pink.
2. Place the crust on a lightly greased 12-in. pizza pan. Spread with pesto; top with the chicken, tomato, beans and cheeses. Bake at 400° for 10-12 minutes or until cheese is melted.

Freeze option: Securely wrap and freeze unbaked pizza. To use, unwrap pizza; bake as directed, increasing time as necessary.
1 piece: 431 cal., 18g fat (6g sat. fat), 65mg chol., 692mg sod., 35g carb. (1g sugars, 1g fiber), 32g pro.

SIMMERED TURKEY
SOFT TACOS

SIMMERED TURKEY SOFT TACOS

I discovered a great way to serve economical turkey thighs. I simmer them in tomato sauce, green chiles and seasonings until they're tender and flavorful, then serve them in tortillas with our favorite fresh toppings.
—*Stella Schams, Tempe, AZ*

PREP: 10 min. • **COOK:** 6 hours
MAKES: 4 servings

- 2 lbs. turkey thighs or drumsticks
- 1 can (8 oz.) tomato sauce
- 1 can (4 oz.) chopped green chiles
- ⅓ cup chopped onion
- 2 Tbsp. Worcestershire sauce
- 1 to 2 Tbsp. chili powder
- ¼ tsp. garlic powder
- 8 flour tortillas (6 in.), warmed
  Optional toppings: Chopped green onions, sliced ripe olives, chopped tomatoes, shredded cheddar cheese, sour cream and shredded lettuce

1. Remove skin from turkey; place turkey in a 5-qt. slow cooker. In a small bowl, combine the tomato sauce, chiles, onion, Worcestershire sauce, chili powder and garlic powder; pour over turkey. Cover and cook on low until turkey is tender, 6-8 hours.
2. Remove turkey; shred meat with 2 forks and return to the slow cooker. Heat through.
3. Spoon about ½ cup turkey mixture down the center of each tortilla. Fold bottom of tortilla over filling and roll up. Add toppings of your choice.

Freeze option: Individually wrap cooled tacos in paper towels and foil; freeze in a freezer container. To use, remove foil; place paper towel-wrapped taco on a microwave-safe plate. Microwave on high until heated through, 3-4 minutes, turning once. Let stand 20 seconds.
2 tacos: 497 cal., 20g fat (4g sat. fat), 114mg chol., 1028mg sod., 34g carb. (3g sugars, 2g fiber), 45g pro.

SLOW-COOKED HERBED TURKEY

I prepare this dish when herbs are plentiful in my garden. The turkey stays moist in the slow cooker and bursts with fresh herb flavors. Everyone in our Bible study potluck group wanted the recipe!
—Sue Jurack, Mequon, WI

- -

PREP: 15 min. + marinating
COOK: 4 hours + standing
MAKES: 16 servings

- 1 can (14½ oz.) chicken broth
- ½ cup lemon juice
- ¼ cup packed brown sugar
- ¼ cup minced fresh sage
- ¼ cup minced fresh thyme
- ¼ cup lime juice
- ¼ cup cider vinegar
- ¼ cup olive oil
- 1 envelope onion soup mix
- 2 Tbsp. Dijon mustard
- 1 Tbsp. minced fresh marjoram
- 1½ tsp. paprika
- 1 tsp. garlic powder
- 1 tsp. pepper
- ½ tsp. salt
- 2 boneless skinless turkey breast halves (3 lbs. each)

1. For marinade, in a blender, combine all ingredients except turkey; cover and process until blended. Pour half the marinade into a bowl; cover and refrigerate. Place turkey breasts in a large, shallow bowl; add remaining marinade. Turn to coat. Cover and refrigerate overnight, turning occasionally.

2. Drain turkey, discarding marinade. Transfer turkey breasts to a 5-qt. slow cooker. Add reserved marinade; cover and cook on high until a thermometer reads 165°, 4-5 hours. Let stand for 10 minutes before slicing.

5 oz. cooked turkey: 232 cal., 5g fat (1g sat. fat), 97mg chol., 369mg sod., 4g carb. (3g sugars, 0 fiber), 40g pro. **Diabetic exchanges:** 5 lean meat, ½ fat.

MAPLE MUSTARD CHICKEN

My husband loves this chicken dish. It calls for only five ingredients, and we try to have them all on hand for a delicious and cozy dinner anytime.
—Jennifer Seidel, Midland, MI

- -

PREP: 5 min. • **COOK:** 3 hours
MAKES: 6 servings

- 6 boneless skinless chicken breast halves (6 oz. each)
- ½ cup maple syrup
- ⅓ cup stone-ground mustard
- 2 Tbsp. quick-cooking tapioca
  Hot cooked brown rice

Place chicken in a 3-qt. slow cooker. In a small bowl, combine the syrup, mustard and tapioca; pour over chicken. Cover and cook on low for 3-4 hours or until tender. Serve with rice.

Freeze option: Cool chicken in sauce. Freeze in freezer containers. To use, partially thaw in refrigerator overnight. Heat through slowly in a covered skillet until a thermometer inserted in chicken reads 165°, stirring occasionally; add broth or water if necessary.

1 chicken breast half: 289 cal., 4g fat (1g sat. fat), 94mg chol., 296mg sod., 24g carb. (17g sugars, 2g fiber), 35g pro.

SLOW-COOKED
HERBED TURKEY

TWO-FOR-ONE
CHICKEN TETRAZZINI

❄ TWO-FOR-ONE CHICKEN TETRAZZINI

A good friend shared a version of this recipe with me 35 years ago. I pay it forward by bringing the second casserole to friends when they are unable to cook.
—*Helen McPhee, Savoy, IL*

PREP: 30 min. • **BAKE:** 20 min.
MAKES: 2 casseroles (4 servings each)

- 1 pkg. (12 oz.) spaghetti
- ⅓ cup butter, cubed
- ⅓ cup all-purpose flour
- ¾ tsp. salt
- ¼ tsp. white pepper
- 1 can (14½ oz.) chicken broth
- 1½ cups half-and-half cream
- 1 cup heavy whipping cream
- 4 cups cubed cooked chicken
- 3 cans (4 oz. each) mushroom stems and pieces, drained
- 1 jar (4 oz.) sliced pimientos, drained
- ½ cup grated Parmesan cheese

1. Cook spaghetti according to package directions. Meanwhile, in a Dutch oven, melt butter. Stir in the flour, salt and pepper until smooth. Gradually add the broth, half-and-half and whipping cream. Bring to a boil; cook and stir until thickened, about 2 minutes.
2. Remove from the heat. Stir in the chicken, mushrooms and pimientos. Drain spaghetti; add to the chicken mixture and toss to coat.
3. Transfer to 2 greased 11x7-in. baking dishes. Sprinkle with the Parmesan. Cover and freeze 1 casserole for up to 2 months. Bake the second casserole, uncovered, at 350° until heated through, 20-25 minutes.
To use frozen casserole: Thaw in the refrigerator overnight. Cover and bake at 350° for 30 minutes. Uncover; bake until heated through, 15-20 minutes more. Stir before serving.
1 cup: 576 cal., 30g fat (17g sat. fat), 144mg chol., 814mg sod., 41g carb. (4g sugars, 2g fiber), 31g pro.

SAUCY INDIAN-STYLE
CHICKEN & VEGETABLES

❄ 🍲 SAUCY INDIAN-STYLE CHICKEN & VEGETABLES

This easy Indian dish will be loved by all. Feel free to add more or less tikka masala sauce according to your taste.
—*Erica Polly, Sun Prairie, WI*

PREP: 15 min. • **COOK:** 4 hours
MAKES: 8 servings

- 2 medium sweet potatoes, peeled and cut into 1½-in. pieces
- 2 Tbsp. water
- 2 medium sweet red peppers, cut into 1-in. pieces
- 3 cups fresh cauliflowerets
- 2 lbs. boneless skinless chicken thighs, cubed
- 2 jars (15 oz. each) tikka masala curry sauce
- ¾ tsp. salt
  Minced fresh cilantro, optional
  Naan flatbreads, warmed

1. Microwave sweet potatoes and water, covered, on high just until potatoes begin to soften, 3-4 minutes.
2. In a 5- or 6-qt. slow cooker, combine vegetables and chicken; add sauce and salt. Cook, covered, on low 4-5 hours or until meat is tender. If desired, top with cilantro. Serve with warmed naan.
Freeze option: Omitting cilantro, freeze cooled chicken and vegetable mixture in freezer containers. To use, partially thaw in refrigerator overnight. Microwave, covered, on high in a microwave-safe dish until heated through, stirring gently as needed; add water if necessary. If desired, top with cilantro. Serve with warmed naan.
1¼ cups: 334 cal., 15g fat (4g sat. fat), 80mg chol., 686mg sod., 25g carb. (12g sugars, 5g fiber), 25g pro. **Diabetic exchanges:** 3 lean meat, 2 fat, 1½ starch.

BOMBAY CHICKEN

This grilled chicken dinner always turns out moist and tender. The marinade has a slightly exotic flair, giving the dish a zesty flavor. It makes a beautiful presentation as well.
—*June Thomas, Chesterton, IN*

PREP: 10 min. + marinating • **GRILL:** 20 min.
MAKES: 8 servings

- 1½ cups plain yogurt
- ¼ cup lemon juice
- 2 Tbsp. chili powder
- 2 Tbsp. paprika
- 2 Tbsp. olive oil
- 1½ tsp. salt
- ½ to 1 tsp. cayenne pepper
- ½ tsp. garlic powder
- ¼ tsp. ground ginger
- ¼ tsp. ground cardamom
- ⅛ tsp. ground cinnamon
- 4 to 5 lbs. bone-in chicken thighs and legs, skin removed

1. In a large shallow dish, combine all ingredients but chicken. Add the chicken; turn to coat. Refrigerate, covered, overnight.
2. Drain chicken, discarding marinade.
3. On a lightly oiled grill rack, grill the chicken, covered, over medium-hot heat 10-15 minutes on each side or until a thermometer reads 170°-175°.
4 oz. cooked chicken: 255 cal., 13g fat (3g sat. fat), 106mg chol., 344mg sod., 3g carb. (0 sugars, 1g fiber), 31g pro.

❄ FAVORITE CHICKEN POTPIE

Chock-full of chicken, potatoes, peas and corn, this autumn favorite makes two golden pies, so you can serve one at supper and save the other for a busy night. These potpies are perfect for company or a potluck.
—*Karen Johnson, Bakersfield, CA*

PREP: 40 min. • **BAKE:** 35 min. + standing
MAKES: 2 potpies (8 servings each)

- 2 cups diced peeled potatoes
- 1¾ cups sliced carrots
- 1 cup butter, cubed
- ⅔ cup chopped onion
- 1 cup all-purpose flour
- 1¾ tsp. salt
- 1 tsp. dried thyme
- ¾ tsp. pepper
- 3 cups chicken broth
- 1½ cups whole milk
- 4 cups cubed cooked chicken
- 1 cup frozen peas
- 1 cup frozen corn
- 4 sheets refrigerated pie crust

1. Preheat oven to 425°. Place potatoes and carrots in a large saucepan; add water to cover. Bring to a boil. Reduce heat; cook, covered, 8-10 minutes or until crisp-tender; drain.
2. In a large skillet, heat butter over medium-high heat. Add onion; cook and stir until tender. Stir in flour and seasonings until blended. Gradually stir in broth and milk. Bring to a boil, stirring constantly; cook and stir 2 minutes or until thickened. Stir in the chicken, peas, corn and potato-carrot mixture; remove from heat.
3. Unroll a pie crust into each of two 9-in. pie plates; trim even with rims of plates. Add chicken mixture. Unroll remaining crusts; place over filling. Trim, seal and flute edges. Cut slits in the tops.
4. Bake 35-40 minutes or until crust is lightly browned. Let stand 15 minutes before cutting.
Freeze option: Cover and freeze the unbaked pies. To use, remove from freezer 30 minutes before baking (do not thaw). Preheat oven to 425°. Place pies on baking sheets; cover edges loosely with foil. Bake 30 minutes. Reduce oven setting to 350°; bake 70-80 minutes longer or until crust is golden brown and a thermometer inserted in center reads 165°.
1 serving: 475 cal., 28g fat (14g sat. fat), 74mg chol., 768mg sod., 41g carb. (5g sugars, 2g fiber), 15g pro.

FAVORITE
CHICKEN POTPIE

OVEN-FRIED CHICKEN DRUMSTICKS

OVEN-FRIED CHICKEN DRUMSTICKS

This fabulous recipe uses Greek yogurt to create an amazing marinade that makes the chicken incredibly moist. No one will guess that it's been lightened up and not even fried!
—*Kimberly Wallace, Dennison, OH*

- -

PREP: 20 min. + marinating • **BAKE:** 40 min.
MAKES: 4 servings

1	cup fat-free plain Greek yogurt
1	Tbsp. Dijon mustard
2	garlic cloves, minced
8	chicken drumsticks (4 oz. each), skin removed
½	cup whole wheat flour
1½	tsp. paprika
1	tsp. baking powder
1	tsp. salt
1	tsp. pepper
	Olive oil-flavored cooking spray

1. In a large bowl or dish, combine yogurt, mustard and garlic. Add chicken; turn to coat. Cover; refrigerate 8 hours or overnight.

2. Preheat oven to 425°. In another bowl, mix flour, paprika, baking powder, salt and pepper. Remove chicken from the marinade and add, 1 piece at a time, to flour mixture; toss to coat. Place on a wire rack over a baking sheet; spritz with cooking spray. Bake 40-45 minutes or until a thermometer inserted into the chicken reads 170°-175°.

2 drumsticks: 227 cal., 7g fat (1g sat. fat), 81mg chol., 498mg sod., 9g carb. (2g sugars, 1g fiber), 31g pro. **Diabetic exchanges:** 4 lean meat, ½ starch.

TEST KITCHEN TIP
To prepare in air fryer, preheat air fryer to 375°. Working in batches if necessary, place coated chicken in a single layer in air-fryer basket sprayed with cooking spray. Air-fry until a thermometer reads 170°, about 20 minutes, turning chicken halfway through cooking. Repeat. When the last batch is cooked, return all chicken to the basket and air-fry 2-3 minutes to heat through.

❄ MAKE-AHEAD SAUCY SANDWICHES

I've made these sandwiches many times for luncheons and light dinners. They can be prepared ahead of time and popped in the oven when needed.
—*Elizabeth Rothert, Kernville, CA*

- -

PREP: 15 min. + freezing • **BAKE:** 50 min.
MAKES: 12 sandwiches

24	slices white sandwich bread
1½	cups diced cooked chicken
1	can (10¾ oz.) condensed cream of mushroom soup, undiluted
½	cup prepared chicken gravy
1	can (8 oz.) water chestnuts, drained and chopped
1	jar (2 oz.) chopped pimientos, drained
2	Tbsp. chopped green onions
	Salt and pepper to taste
5	large eggs
⅓	cup 2% milk
2	bags (6 oz. each) ridged potato chips, crushed

Trim crusts from bread. (Discard or save crusts for another use.) In a medium bowl, combine the chicken, soup, gravy, chopped water chestnuts, pimientos, onions, salt and pepper. Spread mixture on 12 slices of bread; top with remaining 12 bread slices. Wrap each sandwich in foil and freeze.

To prepare frozen sandwiches: In a shallow bowl, beat eggs and milk. Unwrap sandwiches; dip frozen sandwiches in egg mixture and then in the crushed potato chips. Place on greased baking sheets. Bake at 325° for 50-60 minutes or until golden brown.

1 sandwich: 385 cal., 17g fat (5g sat. fat), 96mg chol., 702mg sod., 44g carb. (5g sugars, 3g fiber), 14g pro.

GRILLED HULI HULI CHICKEN

I got this grilled chicken recipe from a friend while living in Hawaii. The dish sizzles with the flavors of ginger, soy sauce and brown sugar. *Huli* means "turn" in Hawaiian. The sweet and savory glaze is fantastic on pork chops, too.
—*Sharon Boling, San Diego, CA*

PREP: 15 min. + marinating • **GRILL:** 15 min.
MAKES: 12 servings

1	cup packed brown sugar
¾	cup ketchup
¾	cup reduced-sodium soy sauce
⅓	cup sherry or chicken broth
2½	tsp. minced fresh gingerroot
1½	tsp. minced garlic
24	boneless skinless chicken thighs (about 6 lbs.)

1. In a small bowl, mix all ingredients except chicken. Reserve 1⅓ cups for basting; cover and refrigerate. Divide remaining marinade between 2 large shallow dishes. Add 12 thighs to each dish; turn to coat. Refrigerate, covered, for 8 hours or overnight.

2. Drain chicken, discarding marinade.

3. Grill chicken, covered, on an oiled rack over medium heat for 6-8 minutes on each side or until a thermometer inserted into the chicken reads 170°; baste occasionally with reserved marinade during the last 5 minutes.

2 chicken thighs: 391 cal., 16g fat (5g sat. fat), 151mg chol., 651mg sod., 15g carb. (14g sugars, 0 fiber), 43g pro.

TEST KITCHEN TIPS

- Use any cut of chicken you'd like but for grilling, we love the moistness of chicken thighs. They're economical, too.
- Transport yourself to Hawaii without firing up the grill! Pat marinated chicken dry with paper towels; sear in a touch of oil in a skillet or grill pan. Transfer to a 375° oven for basting and baking.

GRILLED HULI HULI
CHICKEN

CRANBERRY CHIPOTLE
CHICKEN ENCHILADAS

CRANBERRY CHIPOTLE CHICKEN ENCHILADAS

Whether canned or homemade, cranberry sauce delivers a healthy dose of vitamins to this dish. A little bit sweet, a little bit smoky, these enchiladas are a delightful way to use leftover chicken or turkey.

—*Julie Peterson, Crofton, MD*

PREP: 30 min. • **BAKE:** 30 min.
MAKES: 8 enchiladas

2½ **cups shredded cooked chicken or turkey**
1   **can (15 oz.) black beans, rinsed and drained**
1   **cup (4 oz.) shredded reduced-fat Colby-Monterey Jack cheese, divided**
1   **can (14 oz.) whole-berry cranberry sauce, divided**
½   **cup reduced-fat sour cream**
1½ **cups salsa, divided**
4   **green onions, sliced**
¼   **cup minced fresh cilantro**
1   **to 2 Tbsp. finely chopped chipotle peppers in adobo sauce**
1   **tsp. ground cumin**
1   **tsp. chili powder**
½   **tsp. pepper**

8   **whole wheat tortilla or flour tortillas (8 in.), warmed**

1. Preheat oven to 350°. In a medium bowl, combine chicken, beans, ¾ cup shredded cheese, ⅔ cup cranberry sauce, sour cream, ½ cup salsa, green onions, cilantro, chipotle peppers, cumin, chili powder and pepper. Place ¾ cup chicken mixture off center on each tortilla. Roll up and place in a greased 13x9-in. baking dish, seam side down.
2. Combine the remaining salsa and cranberry sauce; pour over enchiladas. Cover and bake 25 minutes. Uncover; sprinkle with remaining ¼ cup cheese. Bake 5-10 minutes longer or until cheese is melted.

To Make Ahead: Cover and refrigerate unbaked enchiladas overnight. Remove from refrigerator 30 minutes before baking. Preheat oven to 350°. Cover dish with foil; bake as directed, increasing covered time to 35-40 minutes or until heated through and a thermometer inserted in center reads 165°. Uncover; sprinkle with remaining ¼ cup cheese. Bake 5-10 minutes longer or until cheese is melted.

1 enchilada: 368 cal., 6g fat (3g sat. fat), 53mg chol., 623mg sod., 54g carb. (15g sugars, 6g fiber), 24g pro

ASIAN-STYLE MEAT LOAF

Here's a family-friendly meat loaf with a hint of Asian flair. Serve it with sugar snap peas or steamed baby bok choy and brown rice.
—Taste of Home *Test Kitchen*

PREP: 25 min. • **BAKE:** 50 min. + standing
MAKES: 2 loaves (8 pieces each)

- 1⅓ cups panko bread crumbs
- 1 small onion, finely chopped
- 2 large eggs, lightly beaten
- ⅓ cup 2% milk
- ¼ cup hoisin sauce
- 1 Tbsp. reduced-sodium soy sauce
- 2 garlic cloves, minced
- 2 tsp. prepared mustard
- 1¼ tsp. ground ginger
- 1 tsp. salt
- 2 lbs. extra-lean ground turkey
- 1 lb. Italian turkey sausage links, casings removed

TOPPING
- 1 cup ketchup
- ½ cup packed brown sugar
- 2 tsp. prepared mustard

1. Preheat oven to 350°. In a large bowl, combine first 10 ingredients. Add turkey and sausage; mix lightly but thoroughly. Transfer to 2 greased 9x5-in. loaf pans. Mix topping ingredients; spread over tops.
2. Bake 50-55 minutes or until a thermometer reads 165°. Let stand 10 minutes before slicing.
Freeze option: In plastic wrap-lined loaf pans, shape meat loaves. Cover; freeze until firm. Remove from pans and wrap securely in foil; return to freezer. To use, unwrap and bake meat loaves as directed, increasing time to 1¼-1½ hours or until a thermometer inserted in center reads 165°.
1 piece: 187 cal., 6g fat (1g sat. fat), 67mg chol., 636mg sod., 17g carb. (12g sugars, trace fiber), 16g pro. **Diabetic exchanges:** 2 lean meat, 1 starch.

READER REVIEW

"Really good! I cut this recipe in half and instead of 1 big meat loaf, made 8 mini meat loaves. I served them with a fried rice that had plenty of vegetables."

PRPLMONKY5, TASTEOFHOME.COM

THAI CHICKEN & SLAW

THAI CHICKEN & SLAW

With a hint of sweetness from the honey, this zesty recipe has become very popular with my friends and family. I make it whenever I have visitors.
—*Karen Norris, Philadelphia, PA*

PREP: 25 min. + marinating • **COOK:** 30 min.
MAKES: 8 servings

- ½ cup canola oil
- ½ cup white wine vinegar
- ½ cup honey
- 2 Tbsp. minced fresh gingerroot
- 2 Tbsp. reduced-sodium soy sauce
- 2 garlic cloves, minced
- 1 tsp. sesame oil
- 8 boneless skinless chicken thighs (about 2 lbs.)

SLAW
- 6 cups coleslaw mix
- 1 cup frozen shelled edamame, thawed
- 1 medium sweet red pepper, chopped
- 1 Tbsp. creamy peanut butter
- ½ tsp. salt
- 4 green onions, sliced

1. In a small bowl, whisk the first 7 ingredients until blended. Pour 1 cup marinade into a bowl or shallow dish. Add chicken and turn to coat. Cover and refrigerate overnight. Cover and refrigerate remaining marinade.
2. Preheat oven to 350°. Drain chicken, discarding marinade from the bowl. Place chicken in a 13x9-in. baking dish coated with cooking spray. Bake, uncovered, until a thermometer inserted into chicken reads 170°, 30-40 minutes.
3. Meanwhile, place coleslaw mix, edamame and chopped peppers in a large bowl. Add peanut butter and salt to reserved marinade; whisk until blended. Pour over the coleslaw mixture; toss to coat. Refrigerate until serving.
4. Serve chicken with slaw. Sprinkle with sliced green onions.
3 oz. cooked chicken with ⅔ cup slaw: 326 cal., 18g fat (3g sat. fat), 76mg chol., 171mg sod., 16g carb. (12g sugars, 2g fiber), 24g pro. **Diabetic exchanges:** 3 lean meat, 2 fat, 1 vegetable, ½ starch.

CHICKEN MERLOT WITH MUSHROOMS

A dear friend who liked cooking as much as I do shared this recipe with me, and I think of her every time I make it. Friends and family love it and request it often.

—*Shelli McWilliam, Salem, OR*

PREP: 15 min. • **COOK:** 5 hours
MAKES: 8 servings

- ¾ lb. sliced fresh mushrooms
- 1 large onion, chopped
- 2 garlic cloves, minced
- 3 lbs. boneless skinless chicken thighs
- 1 can (6 oz.) tomato paste
- ¾ cup chicken broth
- ¼ cup merlot or additional chicken broth
- 2 Tbsp. quick-cooking tapioca
- 2 tsp. sugar
- 1½ tsp. dried basil
- ½ tsp. salt
- ¼ tsp. pepper
- 2 Tbsp. grated Parmesan cheese
  Hot cooked pasta, optional

1. Place mushrooms, onion and garlic in a 5-qt. slow cooker. Top with chicken.
2. In a small bowl, combine the tomato paste, broth, wine, tapioca, sugar, basil, salt and pepper. Pour over chicken. Cover and cook on low for 5-6 hours or until chicken is tender.
3. Sprinkle with cheese. Serve with pasta if desired.

Freeze option: Freeze cooled chicken mixture in freezer containers. To use, partially thaw in refrigerator overnight. Heat through in a saucepan, stirring occasionally; add broth or water if necessary.

5 oz. cooked chicken with ½ cup sauce: 310 cal., 13g fat (4g sat. fat), 115mg chol., 373mg sod., 11g carb. (5g sugars, 1g fiber), 35g pro.
Diabetic exchanges: 5 lean meat, ½ starch.

Baked Chicken Merlot with Mushrooms: In a greased 3-qt. baking dish, combine mushrooms, onion and garlic. Top with chicken. In a small bowl, combine tomato paste, broth, wine, tapioca, sugar, basil, salt and pepper; pour over chicken. Cover and bake at 325° for 1¼-1½ hours or until chicken is tender. Sprinkle with cheese. Serve with pasta if desired.

CHICKEN MERLOT WITH MUSHROOMS

RANCH-MARINATED CHICKEN BREASTS

The pub favorite of pairing ranch dressing and chicken comes home to your kitchen. With a little prep time the night before, you can have these savory chicken breasts ready in about half an hour.

—*Barbee Decker, Whispering Pines, NC*

PREP: 10 min. + marinating • **BAKE:** 25 min.
MAKES: 6 servings

- 2 cups sour cream
- 1 envelope ranch salad dressing mix
- 4 tsp. lemon juice
- 4 tsp. Worcestershire sauce
- 2 tsp. celery salt
- 2 tsp. paprika
- 1 tsp. garlic salt
- 1 tsp. pepper
- 6 boneless skinless chicken breast halves (6 oz. each)
- ¼ cup butter, melted

1. Combine the first 8 ingredients in a large shallow dish. Add the chicken; turn to coat. Refrigerate, covered, 8 hours or overnight.
2. Drain chicken, discarding marinade. Place chicken in a greased 15x10x1-in. baking pan. Drizzle with butter. Bake, uncovered, at 350° for 25-30 minutes or until a thermometer inserted into chicken reads 165°.
1 chicken breast half: 421 cal., 28g fat (15g sat. fat), 133mg chol., 733mg sod., 5g carb. (3g sugars, 0 fiber), 37g pro.

ZESTY SAUSAGE
& BEANS, P. 65

Pork, Sausage & Ham

These prep-ahead, freezer-friendly meals take the guesswork out of your dinnertime quandaries.

PORK TACOS WITH
MANGO SALSA, P. 69

❄ 🍲 SUPER EASY COUNTRY-STYLE RIBS

I'm a die-hard rib fanatic. When we were growing up, our mom made these for us all the time, and we still can't get enough of them.
—*Stephanie Loaiza, Layton, UT*

PREP: 10 min. • **COOK:** 5 hours
MAKES: 4 servings

- 1½ cups ketchup
- ½ cup packed brown sugar
- ½ cup white vinegar
- 2 tsp. seasoned salt
- ½ tsp. liquid smoke, optional
- 2 lbs. boneless country-style pork ribs

1. In a 3-qt. slow cooker, mix the ketchup, brown sugar, vinegar, seasoned salt and, if desired, liquid smoke. Add ribs; turn to coat. Cook, covered, on low 5-6 hours or until meat is tender.

2. Remove pork to a serving plate. For sauce, skim fat from cooking liquid; transfer liquid to a small saucepan to thicken. Bring to a boil and cook 12-15 minutes or until sauce is reduced to 1½ cups. Serve with ribs.

To Make Ahead: In a large airtight container, combine ketchup, brown sugar, vinegar, seasoned salt and, if desired, liquid smoke. Add pork; cover and freeze. To use, place container in refrigerator 48 hours or until ribs are completely thawed. Cook as directed.

6 oz. cooked pork with about ⅓ cup sauce: 550 cal., 21g fat (8g sat. fat), 131mg chol., 2003mg sod., 51g carb. (51g sugars, 0 fiber), 40g pro.

❄ POLISH CASSEROLE

When I first made this dish, my 2-year-old liked it so much that he wanted it for every meal! You can use almost any pasta that will hold the sauce.
—*Crystal Jo Bruns, Iliff, CO*

PREP: 25 min. • **BAKE:** 45 min.
MAKES: 2 casseroles (6 servings each)

- 4 cups uncooked penne pasta
- 1½ lbs. smoked Polish sausage or kielbasa, cut into ½-in. slices
- 2 cans (10¾ oz. each) condensed cream of mushroom soup, undiluted
- 1 jar (16 oz.) sauerkraut, rinsed and well drained
- 3 cups shredded Swiss cheese, divided
- 1⅓ cups 2% milk
- 4 green onions, chopped
- 2 Tbsp. Dijon mustard
- 4 garlic cloves, minced

1. Preheat oven to 350°. Cook the pasta according to package directions; drain and transfer to a large bowl. Stir in the sausage, soup, sauerkraut, 2 cups cheese, milk, onions, mustard and garlic.

2. Spoon into 2 greased 8-in. square baking dishes; sprinkle with remaining 1 cup cheese. Bake, uncovered, until golden brown and bubbly, 45-50 minutes.

Freeze option: Cover and freeze unbaked casserole up to 3 months. Thaw in the refrigerator overnight. Remove from refrigerator 30 minutes before baking. Preheat oven to 350°. Bake, uncovered, until golden brown and bubbly, 50-55 minutes.

1 cup: 428 cal., 26g fat (11g sat. fat), 69mg chol., 1193mg sod., 28g carb. (4g sugars, 3g fiber), 19g pro.

POLISH CASSEROLE

ZESTY SAUSAGE
& BEANS

CHEESY SCALLOPED POTATOES & HAM

Creamy, cheesy and easy to make, this casserole is the definition of comfort food. The recipe makes two casseroles, so it's great for a crowd; it freezes nicely, too.
—*Salina Bontrager, Kalona, IA*

PREP: 45 min. • **BAKE:** 1¾ hours
MAKES: 2 casseroles (8 servings each)

- 2 cans (10¾ oz. each) condensed cream of chicken soup, undiluted
- 2 cups sour cream
- ⅔ cup butter, melted
- 1 tsp. garlic powder
- 1 tsp. pepper
- 6½ lbs. potatoes, peeled and cut into ¼-in. slices
- 6 cups cubed fully cooked ham (about 2½ lbs.)
- 1 pkg. (16 oz.) Velveeta, cubed

1. Preheat oven to 350°. Mix first 5 ingredients. Stir in potatoes, ham and cheese. Transfer to 2 greased 13x9-in. baking dishes.
2. Bake, covered, 1 hour. Uncover and bake 45-55 minutes longer or until the potatoes are tender.

Freeze option: Cover and freeze unbaked casseroles. To use, partially thaw in refrigerator overnight. Remove from refrigerator 30 minutes before baking. Preheat oven to 350°. Bake casseroles as directed, increasing time as necessary to heat through until a thermometer inserted in center reads 165°.

1½ cups: 491 cal., 28g fat (15g sat. fat), 106mg chol., 1664mg sod., 34g carb. (5g sugars, 2g fiber), 23g pro.

ZESTY SAUSAGE & BEANS

Your hungry family will love this hearty and delicious dish. Packed with sausage, beans and bacon, it's guaranteed to satisfy the heftiest appetites.
—*Melissa Just, Minneapolis, MN*

PREP: 30 min. • **COOK:** 5 hours
MAKES: 10 servings

- 2 lbs. smoked kielbasa or Polish sausage, halved and sliced
- 2 cans (15 oz. each) black beans, rinsed and drained
- 1 can (15 oz.) great northern beans, rinsed and drained
- 1 can (15 oz.) thick and zesty tomato sauce
- 1 medium green pepper, chopped
- 1 medium onion, chopped
- ½ cup water
- 5 bacon strips, cooked and crumbled
- 3 Tbsp. brown sugar
- 2 Tbsp. cider vinegar
- 3 garlic cloves, minced
- ¼ tsp. dried thyme
- ¼ tsp. dried marjoram
- ¼ tsp. cayenne pepper
  Hot cooked rice

In a large skillet, brown the sausage. Transfer to a 4-qt. slow cooker; add the beans, tomato sauce, green pepper, onion, water, bacon, brown sugar, vinegar, garlic, thyme, marjoram and cayenne. Cover and cook on low 5-6 hours or until vegetables are tender. Serve with rice.

Freeze option: Freeze the cooled sausage mixture in freezer containers. To use, partially thaw in refrigerator overnight. Heat through in a saucepan, stirring occasionally; add broth or water if necessary.

¾ cup: 439 cal., 26g fat (9g sat. fat), 64mg chol., 1505mg sod., 29g carb. (7g sugars, 7g fiber), 20g pro.

READER REVIEW

"This was awesome! The flavors mingled just right. Try zesty spaghetti sauce instead of zesty tomato sauce."

PICHARKIN, TASTEOFHOME.COM

SLOW-COOKER ARIZONA POBLANO PORK

❄ 🍲 SLOW-COOKER ARIZONA POBLANO PORK

We're very fond of Arizona's seasonal poblano peppers, and we love this simple dish that features them. It's great with rice and beans or in a taco with hot sauce.
—*Johnna Johnson, Scottsdale, AZ*

- -

PREP: 20 min. • **COOK:** 3 hours
MAKES: 8 servings

- 1 boneless pork loin roast (3 to 4 lbs.)
- 3 Tbsp. fajita seasoning mix, divided
- 1 Tbsp. olive oil
- 1 can (14½ oz.) fire-roasted diced tomatoes, undrained
- 1 large red onion, chopped
- 1½ cups chopped seeded fresh poblano peppers
- ¼ cup beef broth
- 1 tsp. chili powder
- ¾ tsp. ground cumin
- ½ tsp. garlic powder
- ½ tsp. cayenne pepper
- Optional: Hot cooked rice and chipotle hot sauce

1. Sprinkle roast with 2 Tbsp. fajita seasoning. In a large skillet, heat oil over medium heat; brown meat. Transfer meat to a 5- or 6-qt. slow cooker. In a large bowl, combine the next 8 ingredients and remaining 1 Tbsp. fajita seasoning; pour over meat. Cook, covered, on low until a thermometer inserted in pork reads at least 145°, about 3 hours.
2. Remove roast; cool slightly. Cut pork into bite-sized pieces; return to slow cooker. Heat through. If desired, serve pork with rice and hot sauce.

Freeze option: Place cubed roast in freezer containers; top with cooking juices. Cool and freeze. To use, partially thaw in refrigerator overnight. Heat through in a saucepan, stirring occasionally.

1¼ cups: 274 cal., 10g fat (3g sat. fat), 85mg chol., 588mg sod., 10g carb. (4g sugars, 1g fiber), 34g pro.

❄ BREADSTICK PIZZA

Make Monday into "Fun-day" with hassle-free homemade pizza featuring refrigerated breadsticks as the crust. Feeding kids? Slice pieces into small strips and let them dip each strip into marinara sauce. They'll love it!
—*Mary Hankins, Kansas City, MO*

- -

PREP: 25 min. • **BAKE:** 20 min.
MAKES: 12 servings

- 2 tubes (11 oz. each) refrigerated breadsticks
- ½ lb. sliced fresh mushrooms
- 2 medium green peppers, chopped
- 1 medium onion, chopped
- 1½ tsp. Italian seasoning, divided
- 4 tsp. olive oil, divided
- 1½ cups shredded cheddar cheese, divided
- 5 oz. Canadian bacon, chopped
- 1½ cups shredded part-skim mozzarella cheese
- Marinara sauce

1. Unroll breadsticks into a greased 15x10x1-in. baking pan. Press onto the bottom and up the sides of pan; pinch seams to seal. Bake at 350° until set, 6-8 minutes.
2. Meanwhile, in a large skillet, cook and stir mushrooms, peppers, onion and 1 tsp. Italian seasoning in 2 tsp. oil until crisp-tender; drain.
3. Brush crust with remaining 2 tsp. oil. Sprinkle with ¾ cup cheddar cheese; top with vegetable mixture and Canadian bacon. Combine mozzarella cheese and remaining ¾ cup cheddar cheese; sprinkle over top. Sprinkle with remaining ½ tsp. seasoning.
4. Bake until cheese is melted and crust is golden brown, 20-25 minutes. Serve with marinara sauce.

Freeze option: Bake crust as directed; add toppings and cool. Securely wrap and freeze unbaked pizza. To use, unwrap pizza and bake as directed, increasing time as necessary.

1 piece: 267 cal., 11g fat (6g sat. fat), 27mg chol., 638mg sod., 29g carb. (5g sugars, 2g fiber), 13g pro.

BREADSTICK
PIZZA

HAM & PINEAPPLE KABOBS

For a twist on the usual holiday fare, my family turns ham and pineapple into juicy kabobs. The marinade gets its unique zip from hoisin, teriyaki and soy sauces.
—*Chandra Lane Sirois, Kansas City, MO*

- -

PREP: 30 min. + marinating • **BAKE:** 15 min.
MAKES: 12 servings

¼ cup hoisin sauce
¼ cup unsweetened pineapple juice
¼ cup teriyaki sauce
1 Tbsp. honey
1½ tsp. rice vinegar
1½ tsp. reduced-sodium soy sauce
KABOBS
2 lbs. fully cooked boneless ham, cut into 1-in. pieces
1 large fresh pineapple, peeled, cored and cut into 1-in. cubes (about 4 cups)

1. In a large shallow dish, combine the first 6 ingredients. Add ham; turn to coat. Cover; refrigerate overnight.

2. Preheat oven to 350°. Drain ham, reserving marinade. For glaze, pour marinade into a small saucepan; bring to a boil. Reduce heat; simmer, uncovered, until slightly thickened, 5-7 minutes, stirring occasionally. Remove from heat.

3. Meanwhile, on 12 metal or soaked wooden skewers, alternately thread ham and pineapple; place in a foil-lined 15x10x1-in. baking pan. Brush with glaze. Bake, uncovered, until lightly browned, 15-20 minutes.

1 kabob: 144 cal., 3g fat (1g sat. fat), 39mg chol., 1109mg sod., 15g carb. (12g sugars, 1g fiber), 15g pro.

HAM & CHEESE CASSEROLES

❄ HAM & CHEESE CASSEROLES

I got this recipe from my mother. I love it because it's easy and I've usually got the ingredients on hand. Also, it freezes well and I can have it handy when extra guests show up. Everyone always likes this dish—there are never leftovers.
—*Jan Schoshke, Brookville, KS*

- -

PREP: 20 min. • **BAKE:** 25 min.
MAKES: 2 casseroles (8 servings each)

1½ lbs. uncooked egg noodles
3 lbs. cubed fully cooked ham
4 cans (10¾ oz. each) condensed cream of chicken soup, undiluted
4 cups frozen cut green beans, thawed
1 cup 2% milk
¼ cup butter, melted
2 cups shredded Colby-Monterey Jack cheese

1. Preheat oven to 350°. Cook pasta according to package directions.

2. Meanwhile, in a large bowl, combine ham, soup, beans and milk. Drain pasta; pour over ham mixture and toss to coat. Transfer to 2 greased 13x9-in. baking dishes.

3. Drizzle each with butter; sprinkle with cheese. Bake, uncovered, 25-30 minutes or until heated through.

Freeze option: Cool unbaked casseroles; cover and freeze up to 3 months. To use, partially thaw in refrigerator overnight. Remove from refrigerator 30 minutes before baking. Preheat oven to 350°. Bake, uncovered, 40-45 minutes or until heated through and a thermometer inserted in center reads 165°.

1⅓ cups: 470 cal., 21g fat (9g sat. fat), 109mg chol., 1786mg sod., 42g carb. (3g sugars, 3g fiber), 27g pro.

PORK TACOS WITH MANGO SALSA

I've made quite a few tacos in my day, but you can't beat the tender filling made in a slow cooker. These are by far the best pork tacos we've had—and we've tried plenty. Make the mango salsa from scratch if you have time! Yum.
—Amber Massey, Argyle, TX

PREP: 25 min. • **COOK:** 6 hours
MAKES: 12 servings

- 2 Tbsp. lime juice
- 2 Tbsp. white vinegar
- 3 Tbsp. chili powder
- 2 tsp. ground cumin
- 1½ tsp. salt
- ½ tsp. pepper
- 3 cups cubed fresh pineapple
- 1 small red onion, coarsely chopped
- 2 chipotle peppers in adobo sauce
- 1 bottle (12 oz.) dark Mexican beer
- 3 lbs. pork tenderloin, cut into 1-in. cubes
- ¼ cup chopped fresh cilantro
- 1 jar (16 oz.) mango salsa
- 24 corn tortillas (6 in.), warmed
  Optional: Cubed fresh pineapple, chopped avocado and queso fresco

1. Puree the first 9 ingredients in a blender; stir in beer. In a 5- or 6-qt. slow cooker, combine pork and pineapple mixture. Cook, covered, on low until pork is very tender, 6-8 hours. Stir to break up pork.
2. Stir cilantro into salsa. Using a slotted spoon, serve pork mixture in tortillas; add salsa and toppings as desired.

Freeze option: Freeze cooled meat mixture and cooking juices in freezer containers. To use, partially thaw in refrigerator overnight. Heat through in a saucepan, stirring occasionally.

2 tacos: 282 cal., 6g fat (2g sat. fat), 64mg chol., 678mg sod., 30g carb. (5g sugars, 5g fiber), 26g pro. **Diabetic exchanges:** 3 lean meat, 2 starch.

ITALIAN PORK CHOPS

Not only is it easy to use my slow cooker, but the results are fabulous. Meat cooked this way always comes out so tender and juicy. These pork chops are simmered in a thick tomato sauce.
—Bonnie Marlow, Ottoville, OH

PREP: 15 min. • **COOK:** 5 hours
MAKES: 6 servings

- 6 boneless pork loin chops (6 oz. each)
- 1 Tbsp. canola oil
- 1 medium green pepper, diced
- 1 can (6 oz.) tomato paste
- 1 jar (4½ oz.) sliced mushrooms, drained
- ½ cup water
- 1 envelope spaghetti sauce mix
- ½ to 1 tsp. hot pepper sauce

1. In a large skillet, brown pork chops in oil over medium heat 3-4 minutes on each side; drain. In a 5-qt. slow cooker, combine the remaining ingredients. Top with pork chops.
2. Cover and cook on low 5-6 hours or until meat is tender.

Freeze option: Cool pork chop mixture. Freeze in freezer containers. To use, partially thaw in refrigerator overnight. Transfer to a covered skillet and heat through slowly, stirring occasionally, until a thermometer inserted in pork reads 165°.

1 pork chop: 303 cal., 12g fat (4g sat. fat), 82mg chol., 763mg sod., 13g carb. (5g sugars, 3g fiber), 34g pro.

PORK TACOS WITH MANGO SALSA

PULLED PORK SANDWICHES

PULLED PORK SANDWICHES

These simple sandwiches taste like something you'd order from a local barbecue joint. The tender meat basically shreds itself when it's done cooking. This is definitely my favorite pulled pork sandwich of all time.
—Lauren Adamson, Layton, UT

- -

PREP: 15 min. • **COOK:** 8 hours
MAKES: 10 servings

⅓	cup liquid smoke
3	Tbsp. paprika
3	tsp. salt
3	tsp. pepper
1	tsp. garlic powder
1	tsp. ground mustard
1	boneless pork shoulder butt roast (3 to 4 lbs.)
1	bottle (18 oz.) barbecue sauce
10	hamburger buns, split

1. In a small bowl, whisk the first 6 ingredients; rub over roast. Place the roast in a 5- or 6-qt. slow cooker. Cook, covered, on low until meat is tender, 8-10 hours.

2. Remove roast; cool slightly. Discard cooking juices. Shred pork with 2 forks; return to slow cooker. Stir in barbecue sauce; heat through. Serve on buns.

Freeze option: In a small bowl, whisk the first 6 ingredients; rub over roast. Place the roast in a freezer container and freeze. To use, place roast in refrigerator for 48 hours or until completely thawed. Cook and serve as directed.

Freeze option for leftovers: Freeze cooled meat mixture in freezer containers. To use, partially thaw in refrigerator overnight. Heat through in a saucepan, stirring occasionally; add water if necessary.

1 sandwich: 436 cal., 16g fat (5g sat. fat), 81mg chol., 827mg sod., 44g carb. (20g sugars, 2g fiber), 28g pro.

SPICY PORK &
SQUASH RAGU

SPICY PORK & SQUASH RAGU

This recipe is a marvelously spicy combo that's perfect for cooler fall weather and satisfying after a day spent outdoors.
—*Monica Osterhaus, Paducah, KY*

- -

PREP: 20 min. • **COOK:** 5 hours
MAKES: 10 servings

- 2 cans (14½ oz. each) stewed tomatoes, undrained
- 1 pkg. (12 oz.) frozen cooked winter squash, thawed
- 1 large sweet onion, cut into ½-in. pieces
- 1 medium sweet red pepper, cut into ½-in. pieces
- 1½ tsp. crushed red pepper flakes
- 2 lbs. boneless country-style pork ribs
- 1 tsp. salt
- ¼ tsp. garlic powder
- ¼ tsp. pepper
  Hot cooked pasta
  Shaved Parmesan cheese, optional

1. Combine first 5 ingredients in bottom of a 6- or 7-qt. slow cooker. Sprinkle ribs with salt, garlic powder and pepper; place in slow cooker. Cook, covered, on low until pork is tender, 5-6 hours.
2. Remove cover; stir to break pork into smaller pieces. Serve with pasta. If desired, top with Parmesan cheese.
Freeze option: Freeze the cooled sauce in freezer containers. To use, partially thaw in refrigerator overnight. Heat through in a saucepan, stirring occasionally.
1 cup ragu: 195 cal., 8g fat (3g sat. fat), 52mg chol., 426mg sod., 13g carb. (6g sugars, 2g fiber), 17g pro. **Diabetic exchanges:** 2 lean meat, 1 starch.

DID YOU KNOW?
Sweet onions are easy to recognize by their shape. They are shorter from pole to pole and bigger around than regular cooking onions. Many carry the names from the place they're grown, such as Vidalia (from Vidalia, Georgia), Walla Walla (from Washington) and the Maui onion from Hawaii.

SHRIMP & CRAB
CASSEROLE, P. 79

Other Make-Ahead Meals

It's easy to prepare seafood, meatless and other dishes ahead of time. Turn here to learn how.

LOUISIANA JAMBALAYA, P. 75

MUSHROOM MARSALA WITH BARLEY

This filling vegetarian recipe is a tasty mashup of chicken Marsala and mushroom barley soup. It's great as a main dish or a side.
—*Arlene Erlbach, Morton Grove, IL*

PREP: 20 min. • **COOK:** 4¼ hours
MAKES: 6 servings

- 1½ lbs. baby portobello mushrooms, quartered
- 1 cup thinly sliced shallots
- 3 Tbsp. olive oil
- ½ tsp. minced fresh thyme
- ¾ cup Marsala wine, divided
- 3 Tbsp. reduced-fat sour cream
- 2 Tbsp. all-purpose flour
- 1½ tsp. grated lemon zest
- ¼ tsp. salt
- ¼ cup crumbled goat cheese
- ¼ cup minced fresh parsley
- 2½ cups cooked barley

1. In a 4- or 5-qt. slow cooker, combine the mushrooms, shallots, olive oil and thyme. Add ¼ cup Marsala wine. Cook, covered, on low about 4 hours, until vegetables are tender.
2. Stir in sour cream, flour, lemon zest, salt and remaining ½ cup Marsala. Cook, covered, on low 15 minutes longer. Top with goat cheese and parsley. Serve with hot cooked barley.

¾ cup mushrooms with about ⅓ cup barley: 235 cal., 9g fat (2g sat. fat), 7mg chol., 139mg sod., 31g carb. (6g sugars, 5g fiber), 7g pro. **Diabetic exchanges:** 2 starch, 2 fat, 1 vegetable.

RED CLAM SAUCE

RED CLAM SAUCE

This recipe tastes as if it's taken a whole day's work. What a classy way to jazz up pasta sauce!
—*JoAnn Brown, Latrobe, PA*

PREP: 25 min. • **COOK:** 3 hours
MAKES: 4 servings

- 1 medium onion, chopped
- 1 Tbsp. canola oil
- 2 garlic cloves, minced
- 2 cans (6½ oz. each) chopped clams, undrained
- 1 can (14½ oz.) diced tomatoes, undrained
- 1 can (6 oz.) tomato paste
- ¼ cup minced fresh parsley
- 1 bay leaf
- 1 tsp. sugar
- 1 tsp. dried basil
- ½ tsp. dried thyme
- 6 oz. linguine, cooked and drained
  Additional minced fresh parsley, optional

1. In a small skillet, saute onion in oil until tender. Add garlic; cook 1 minute longer.
2. Transfer to a 1½- or 2-qt. slow cooker. Stir in the clams, tomatoes, tomato paste, parsley, bay leaf, sugar, basil and thyme.
3. Cover and cook on low until heated through, 3-4 hours. Discard bay leaf. Serve over linguine. If desired, sprinkle with additional parsley.

Freeze option: Omit additional parsley. Cool before placing in a freezer container. Cover and freeze for up to 3 months. To use, thaw in the refrigerator overnight. Place in a large saucepan; heat through, stirring occasionally. Serve with linguine and, if desired, minced fresh parsley.

1 cup sauce with ¾ cup cooked linguine: 305 cal., 5g fat (0 sat. fat), 15mg chol., 553mg sod., 53g carb. (14g sugars, 7g fiber), 15g pro.

LOUISIANA JAMBALAYA

My husband helped add a little spice to my life. He grew up on Cajun cooking , while I ate mostly meat-and-potato meals.
—*Sandi Pichon, Memphis, TN*

- -

PREP: 10 min. • **COOK:** 30 min.
MAKES: 12 servings

- ¼ cup canola oil
- ½ lb. smoked sausage, halved and sliced
- 2 cups cubed fully cooked ham
- 2 celery ribs, chopped
- 1 large onion, chopped
- 1 medium green pepper, chopped
- 5 green onions, thinly sliced
- 2 garlic cloves, minced
- 1 can (14½ oz.) diced tomatoes, undrained
- 1 tsp. dried thyme
- 1 tsp. salt
- ½ tsp. pepper
- ¼ tsp. cayenne pepper
- 2 cans (14½ oz. each) chicken broth
- 1 cup uncooked long grain rice
- ⅓ cup water
- 4½ tsp. Worcestershire sauce
- 2 lbs. peeled and deveined cooked shrimp (31-40 per lb.)

1. In a Dutch oven, heat oil over medium-high heat. Add sausage and ham; cook and stir until lightly browned. Remove and keep warm. In the drippings, saute the celery, onion, green pepper and green onions until tender. Add the garlic; cook and stir 1 minute longer. Stir in the tomatoes, thyme, salt, pepper and cayenne; cook 5 minutes longer.

2. Stir in broth, rice, water and Worcestershire sauce. Bring to a boil. Reduce the heat; simmer, covered, until rice is tender, about 20 minutes. Stir in the sausage-ham mixture and shrimp; heat through.

Freeze option: Prepare jambalaya as directed, omitting rice and shrimp. Freeze shrimp and the cooled jambalaya in separate freezer containers. Store rice in an airtight container at room temperature. To use, partially thaw jambalaya in refrigerator overnight. Place jambalaya in a 6-qt. stockpot. Bring to a boil; add rice. Reduce heat; simmer, covered, for 10 minutes. Add frozen shrimp; continue cooking until shrimp are heated through and rice is tender, 10-15 minutes.

1 cup: 295 cal., 12g fat (3g sat. fat), 143mg chol., 1183mg sod., 20g carb. (3g sugars, 1g fiber), 25g pro.

LAMB PITAS WITH YOGURT SAUCE

The spiced lamb in these stuffed pita pockets goes perfectly with cool cucumber and yogurt. If you ask me, it's like having your own Greek gyro stand in the kitchen!
—*Angela Leinenbach, Mechanicsville, VA*

- -

PREP: 35 min. • **COOK:** 6 hours
MAKES: 8 servings

- 2 Tbsp. olive oil
- 2 lbs. lamb stew meat (¾-in. pieces)
- 1 large onion, chopped
- 1 garlic clove, minced
- ⅓ cup tomato paste
- ½ cup dry red wine
- 1¼ tsp. salt, divided
- 1 tsp. dried oregano
- ½ tsp. dried basil
- 1 medium cucumber
- 1 cup plain yogurt
- 16 pita pocket halves, warmed
- 4 plum tomatoes, sliced

1. In a large skillet, heat oil over medium-high heat; brown lamb in batches. Transfer lamb to a 3- or 4-qt. slow cooker, reserving the drippings in skillet.

2. In drippings, cook and stir onion over medium heat until tender, 4-6 minutes. Add garlic and tomato paste; cook and stir 2 minutes. Stir in wine, 1 tsp. salt, oregano and basil. Add to lamb. Cook, covered, on low until lamb is tender, 6-8 hours.

3. To serve, dice enough cucumber to measure 1 cup. Combine diced cucumber with yogurt and remaining ¼ tsp. salt. Thinly slice the remaining cucumber. Fill pita halves with lamb mixture, tomato slices, cucumber slices and yogurt mixture.

Freeze option: Freeze cooled lamb mixture in freezer containers. To use, partially thaw in refrigerator overnight. Heat through in a saucepan, stirring occasionally; add broth or water if necessary.

2 filled pita halves: 383 cal., 11g fat (3g sat. fat), 78mg chol., 766mg sod., 39g carb. (5g sugars, 3g fiber), 31g pro. **Diabetic exchanges:** 3 lean meat, 2½ starch, 1 fat.

LOUISIANA JAMBALAYA

FIVE-CHEESE
ZITI AL FORNO

FIVE-CHEESE ZITI AL FORNO

After having the five-cheese ziti at Olive Garden restaurant, I tried to make my own homemade version—and I think I got pretty close. I always double this and freeze the second casserole for another meal.

—*Keri Whitney, Castro Valley, CA*

PREP: 20 min. • **BAKE:** 30 min. + standing
MAKES: 12 servings

- 1½ lbs. (about 7½ cups) uncooked ziti or other small tube-shaped pasta
- 2 jars (24 oz. each) marinara sauce
- 1 jar (15 oz.) Alfredo sauce
- 2 cups shredded part-skim mozzarella cheese, divided
- ½ cup reduced-fat ricotta cheese
- ½ cup shredded provolone cheese
- ½ cup grated Romano cheese

TOPPING

- ½ cup grated Parmesan cheese
- ½ cup panko bread crumbs
- 3 garlic cloves, minced
- 2 Tbsp. olive oil
- Optional: Minced fresh parsley or basil

1. Preheat oven to 350°. Cook the pasta according to the package directions for al dente; drain.

2. Meanwhile, in a large saucepan, combine the marinara sauce, the Alfredo sauce, 1 cup mozzarella and the ricotta, provolone and Romano. Cook over medium heat until sauce begins to simmer and cheeses are melted. Stir in cooked pasta; pour mixture into a greased 13x9-in. baking dish. Top with remaining 1 cup mozzarella cheese.

3. In a small bowl, stir together Parmesan, bread crumbs, garlic and olive oil; sprinkle over the pasta.

4. Bake, uncovered, until mixture is bubbly and topping is golden brown, 30-40 minutes. Let stand 10 minutes before serving. Garnish with fresh parsley or basil if desired.

Freeze option: Cool the unbaked casserole; cover and freeze. To use, partially thaw in the refrigerator overnight. Remove from the refrigerator 30 minutes before baking. Preheat oven to 350°. Cover casserole with foil; bake 50 minutes. Uncover; bake until heated through and a thermometer inserted in center reads 165°, 15-20 minutes longer.

1 cup: 449 cal., 15g fat (8g sat. fat), 32mg chol., 960mg sod., 59g carb. (11g sugars, 4g fiber), 21g pro.

MUSHROOM-GOUDA QUICHE

MUSHROOM-GOUDA QUICHE

For a laid-back Sunday brunch, we make a quiche in no time using refrigerated pie crust. Load it up with mushrooms, aromatic arugula and creamy Gouda.

—*Thomas Faglon, Somerset, NJ*

PREP: 15 min. • **BAKE:** 30 min. + standing
MAKES: 6 servings

- 1 sheet refrigerated pie crust
- 4 large eggs
- 1 cup heavy whipping cream
- ¼ tsp. salt
- ¼ tsp. pepper
- 2 cups sliced fresh shiitake mushrooms (about 4 oz.)
- 1 cup shredded Gouda or Monterey Jack cheese
- 1 cup chopped arugula or fresh baby spinach

1. Preheat oven to 350°. Unroll crust into a 9-in. pie plate; flute edge. Refrigerate while preparing filling.

2. In a large bowl, whisk eggs, cream, salt and pepper until blended. Stir in remaining ingredients. Pour into crust.

3. Bake on a lower oven rack 30-35 minutes or until crust is golden brown and a knife inserted in the center comes out clean. Let stand 10 minutes before cutting.

Freeze option: Cover and freeze unbaked quiche. To use, remove from the freezer 30 minutes before baking (do not thaw). Preheat oven to 350°. Place quiche on a baking sheet; cover quiche crust loosely with foil. Bake as directed, increasing time as necessary until a knife inserted in the center comes out clean.

1 piece: 422 cal., 33g fat (18g sat. fat), 207mg chol., 452mg sod., 21g carb. (4g sugars, 1g fiber), 12g pro.

❄ MUFFIN-TIN PIZZAS

I just baked these mini pizzas and the kids are already demanding more. The no-cook pizza sauce and refrigerated dough make this meal a snap on busy nights.
—*Melissa Haines, Valparaiso, IN*

PREP: 25 min. • **BAKE:** 10 min.
MAKES: 16 mini pizzas

- 1   can (15 oz.) tomato sauce
- 1   can (6 oz.) tomato paste
- 1   tsp. dried basil
- ½   tsp. garlic salt
- ¼   tsp. onion powder
- ¼   tsp. sugar
- 1   tube (11 oz.) refrigerated thin pizza crust
- 1½ cups shredded part-skim mozzarella cheese
- ½   cup finely chopped fresh mushrooms
- ½   cup finely chopped fresh broccoli
- 16 slices pepperoni, halved

1. Preheat oven to 425°. In a small bowl, mix the first 6 ingredients.
2. Unroll pizza crust; cut into 16 squares. Press squares onto bottoms and up sides of 16 ungreased muffin cups, allowing corners to hang over the edges.
3. Spoon 1 Tbsp. sauce mixture into each cup. Top with cheese, mushrooms, broccoli and pepperoni. Bake until crusts are golden brown, 10-12 minutes. Serve with remaining sauce mixture, warmed if desired.
Freeze option: Freeze cooled baked pizzas in an airtight container. To use, reheat pizzas on a baking sheet in a preheated 425° oven until heated through.
2 mini pizzas with 2 Tbsp. sauce: 233 cal., 9g fat (4g sat. fat), 16mg chol., 755mg sod., 26g carb. (5g sugars, 2g fiber), 12g pro.

❄ COMFORTING TUNA PATTIES

My grandmother and mother made these tuna patties on Fridays during Lent. I'm not the biggest fan of tuna, but it's perfect in this dish. These patties are even good cold the next day, if there are any leftovers.
—*Ann Marie Eberhart, Gig Harbor, WA*

PREP: 25 min. + chilling • **COOK:** 4 min./batch
MAKES: 6 servings

- 2   Tbsp. butter
- 3   Tbsp. all-purpose flour
- 1   cup evaporated milk
- 1   pouch (6.4 oz.) light tuna in water
- ⅓   cup plus ½ cup dry bread crumbs, divided
- 1   green onion, finely chopped
- 2   Tbsp. lemon juice
- ½   tsp. salt
- ¼   tsp. pepper
      Oil for frying

1. In a small saucepan, melt the butter over medium heat. Stir in the flour until smooth; gradually whisk in evaporated milk. Bring to a boil, stirring constantly; cook and stir until thickened, 2-3 minutes. Remove from heat. Transfer to a small bowl; cool.
2. Stir in the tuna, ⅓ cup bread crumbs, green onion, lemon juice, salt and pepper. Refrigerate, covered, at least 30 minutes.
3. Place remaining ½ cup bread crumbs in a shallow bowl. Drop ⅓ cup tuna mixture into the crumbs. Gently coat with crumbs and shape into a ½-in.-thick patty. Repeat. In a large skillet, heat oil over medium heat. Add patties in batches; cook 2-3 minutes on each side or until golden brown. Drain on paper towels.
Freeze option: Freeze cooled tuna patties in freezer containers, separating layers with waxed paper. To use, reheat tuna patties on a baking sheet in a preheated 325° oven until heated through.
1 tuna patty: 255 cal., 17g fat (5g sat. fat), 34mg chol., 419mg sod., 15g carb. (5g sugars, 1g fiber), 10g pro.

COMFORTING
TUNA PATTIES

CHICKPEA &
POTATO CURRY

SHRIMP & CRAB CASSEROLE

This is a quick and easy recipe that is truly delicious. The melt-in-your-mouth flavors and different textures are comforting yet elegant. This is a great make-ahead dish, too. Just assemble, cover and refrigerate, then bake when ready.
—*Jan Bartley, Evergreen, NC*

PREP: 25 min. • **BAKE:** 40 min.
MAKES: 8 servings

- 2 pkg. (8.8 oz. each) ready-to-serve long grain and wild rice
- ¼ cup butter, cubed
- 2 celery ribs, chopped
- 1 medium onion, chopped
- 3 Tbsp. all-purpose flour
- 1½ cups half-and-half cream
- 1 tsp. seafood seasoning
- ¾ tsp. salt
- ½ tsp. hot pepper sauce
- ¼ tsp. pepper
- 1½ lbs. uncooked shrimp (31-40 per lb.), peeled and deveined
- 2 cans (6 oz. each) lump crabmeat, drained
- 1 cup shredded Colby-Monterey Jack cheese

1. Preheat oven to 350°. Spread rice into a greased 13x9-in. baking dish. In a large skillet, heat the butter over medium-high heat. Add celery and onion; cook and stir 6-8 minutes or until vegetables are tender. Stir in flour until blended; gradually whisk in cream. Bring to a boil, stirring constantly; cook and stir until thickened, 1-2 minutes.
2. Stir in seafood seasoning, salt, pepper sauce and pepper. Fold in shrimp and crab. Spoon over rice. Sprinkle with cheese. Bake, covered, until shrimp turn pink, 40-45 minutes. Let stand 5 minutes.
To Make Ahead: Can be made a day in advance. Prepare recipe as directed, cooling sauce slightly before adding shrimp and crab. Cover and refrigerate overnight. Remove from the refrigerator 30 minutes before baking. Bake as directed.
1 serving: 376 cal., 17g fat (10g sat. fat), 195mg chol., 1127mg sod., 24g carb. (3g sugars, 1g fiber), 29g pro.

CHICKPEA & POTATO CURRY

I make *chana masala*, the classic Indian dish, in my slow cooker. Browning the onion, ginger and garlic first really makes the sauce amazing.
—*Anjana Devasahayam, San Antonio, TX*

PREP: 25 min. • **COOK:** 6 hours
MAKES: 6 servings

- 1 Tbsp. canola oil
- 1 medium onion, chopped
- 2 garlic cloves, minced
- 2 tsp. minced fresh gingerroot
- 2 tsp. ground coriander
- 1 tsp. garam masala
- 1 tsp. chili powder
- ½ tsp. salt
- ½ tsp. ground cumin
- ¼ tsp. ground turmeric
- 1 can (15 oz.) crushed tomatoes
- 2 cans (15 oz. each) chickpeas or garbanzo beans, rinsed and drained
- 1 large baking potato, peeled and cut into ¾-in. cubes
- 2½ cups vegetable stock
- 1 Tbsp. lime juice
  Chopped fresh cilantro
  Hot cooked rice
  Optional: Sliced red onion and lime wedges

1. In a large skillet, heat oil over medium-high heat; saute onion until tender, 2-4 minutes. Add garlic, ginger and dry seasonings; cook and stir 1 minute. Stir in tomatoes; transfer to a 3- or 4-qt. slow cooker.
2. Stir in chickpeas, potato and stock. Cook, covered, on low until potato is tender and flavors are blended, 6-8 hours.
3. Stir in the lime juice; sprinkle with cilantro. Serve with rice and, if desired, red onion and lime wedges.
1¼ cups chickpea curry: 240 cal., 6g fat (0 sat. fat), 0 chol., 767mg sod., 42g carb. (8g sugars, 9g fiber), 8g pro.

MAKE-AHEAD HEARTY
SIX-LAYER SALAD, P. 90

Sides & Salads

Whether you need a dish to pass or simply want to round out a menu, consider these time-saving specialties.

DIJON VEGGIES
WITH COUSCOUS,
P. 86

OVERNIGHT LAYERED LETTUCE SALAD

This layered salad is a family favorite from a church cookbook I've had for 40 years. The bacon adds a fabulous crunch.

—*Mary Brehm, Cape Coral, FL*

- -

PREP: 20 min. + chilling
MAKES: 16 servings (1 cup each)

- 1   medium head iceberg lettuce, torn
- 1   medium green pepper, chopped
- 1   small sweet red pepper, chopped
- 1   medium onion, sliced and separated into rings
- 2   cups frozen peas (about 10 oz.)
- 1   cup mayonnaise
- 2   Tbsp. sugar
- 1   cup shredded cheddar cheese
- 12 bacon strips, cooked and crumbled
- ¾   cup dried cranberries

1. In a 4-qt. or 13x9-in. glass dish, layer the first 5 ingredients. In a small bowl, mix together the mayonnaise and sugar; spoon over salad, spreading to cover.
2. Sprinkle top with cheese, bacon and cranberries. Refrigerate, covered, overnight.
1 cup: 206 cal., 16g fat (4g sat. fat), 19mg chol., 250mg sod., 11g carb. (7g sugars, 2g fiber), 5g pro.

❄ CRISPY POTATO PUFFS

Crunchy cornflakes and sesame seeds surround a velvety potato filling in these adorable puffs. They are the perfect side dish.

—*Eva Tomlinson, Bryan, OH*

- -

PREP: 35 min. • **BAKE:** 10 min.
MAKES: 12 servings (2 puffs each)

- 4   lbs. cubed peeled potatoes (about 11 cups)
- ½   cup 2% milk
- ¼   cup butter, cubed
- 1½   tsp. salt
- ½   cup shredded cheddar cheese
- 1½   cups crushed cornflakes
- 6   Tbsp. sesame seeds, toasted

1. Place potatoes in a large saucepan; add water to cover. Bring to a boil. Reduce heat; cook, uncovered, 10-15 minutes or until tender. Drain; return to pan.

2. Mash potatoes, gradually adding milk, butter and salt; stir in cheese. Transfer to a large bowl; refrigerate, covered, 2 hours or until firm enough to shape.
3. In a shallow dish, combine cornflakes and sesame seeds. Shape potato mixture into 1½-in. balls; roll in cornflake mixture. Place on greased baking sheets. Bake 7-9 minutes or until golden brown.
Freeze option: Place unbaked puffs on baking sheets; cover and freeze until firm. Transfer to freezer containers. Freeze up to 3 months. To use, preheat oven to 400°. Place frozen potato puffs on greased baking sheets. Bake 15-20 minutes or until golden brown and heated through.
2 puffs: 248 cal., 7g fat (4g sat. fat), 16mg chol., 466mg sod., 42g carb. (3g sugars, 3g fiber), 5g pro.

CRISPY POTATO PUFFS

HOMEMADE PIEROGI

1. In a food processor, combine flour and salt; cover and pulse to blend. Add water, eggs and butter; cover and pulse until dough forms a ball, adding an additional 1 to 2 Tbsp. of water or flour if needed. Let rest, covered, 15 to 30 minutes.

2. Place potatoes in a large saucepan and cover with water. Bring to a boil over high heat. Reduce heat; cover and simmer until tender, 10-15 minutes. Meanwhile, in a large skillet over medium-high heat, saute onions in butter until tender; set aside.

3. Drain potatoes. Over very low heat, stir potatoes until steam has evaporated, about 1-2 minutes. Press through a potato ricer or strainer into a large bowl. Stir in cream cheese, salt, pepper and onion mixture.

4. Divide dough into 4 parts. On a lightly floured surface, roll 1 portion of dough to ⅛-in. thickness; cut with a floured 3-in. biscuit cutter. Place 2 tsp. of filling in center of each circle. Moisten edges with water; fold in half and press edges to seal. Repeat with remaining dough and filling.

5. Bring a Dutch oven of water to a boil over high heat; add pierogi in batches. Reduce heat to a gentle simmer; cook until pierogi float to the top and are tender, 1-2 minutes. Remove with a slotted spoon. In a large skillet, saute 4 pierogi and onion in butter until pierogi are lightly browned and heated through; sprinkle with parsley. Repeat with remaining pierogi.

Freeze option: Place cooled pierogi on waxed paper-lined 15x10x1-in. baking pans; freeze until firm. Transfer to an airtight freezer container; freeze up to 3 months. To use, for each serving, in a large skillet, saute 4 pierogi and ¼ cup chopped onion in 1 Tbsp. butter until pierogi are lightly browned and heated through; sprinkle with minced fresh parsley.

4 pierogi: 373 cal., 22g fat (13g sat. fat), 86mg chol., 379mg sod., 38g carb. (3g sugars, 2g fiber), 6g pro.

READER REVIEW

"This was my first attempt making pierogis, and they did not disappoint. I froze the extras."

JUSTMBETH, TASTEOFHOME.COM

❄

HOMEMADE PIEROGI

Pierogi are dumplings stuffed with a filling, often potatoes and cheese, and boiled, then sizzled with butter. They're ideal for potlucks.
—*Diane Gawrys, Manchester, TN*

PREP: 1 hour • **COOK:** 5 min./batch
MAKES: 6 dozen

- 5   cups all-purpose flour
- 1   tsp. salt
- 1   cup water
- 3   large eggs
- ½   cup butter, softened

FILLING
- 4   medium potatoes, peeled and cubed
- 2   medium onions, chopped
- 2   Tbsp. butter
- 5   oz. cream cheese, softened
- ½   tsp. salt
- ½   tsp. pepper

ADDITIONAL INGREDIENTS (FOR EACH SERVING)
- ¼   cup chopped onion
- 1   Tbsp. butter
      Minced fresh parsley

SLOW-COOKED
RATATOUILLE

PARSNIPS & TURNIPS AU GRATIN

You don't need potatoes to make a delicious au gratin dish! Sometimes I even substitute rutabaga for the turnips. I definitely cherish having this recipe in my collection.
—*Priscilla Gilbert, Indian Harbour Beach, FL*

PREP: 20 min. • **BAKE:** 15 min.
MAKES: 8 servings

- 1½ lbs. parsnips, peeled and sliced
- 1¼ lbs. turnips, peeled and sliced
- 1 can (10¾ oz.) reduced-fat reduced-sodium condensed cream of celery soup, undiluted
- 1 cup fat-free milk
- ½ tsp. pepper
- 1 cup shredded sharp cheddar cheese
- ½ cup panko bread crumbs
- 1 Tbsp. butter, melted

1. Place parsnips and turnips in a large saucepan; cover with water. Bring to a boil. Reduce heat; simmer, uncovered, until crisp-tender, 5-7 minutes.
2. Meanwhile, in a small saucepan, combine the soup, milk and pepper. Bring to a boil; reduce heat to low. Stir in cheese until melted. Drain vegetables; transfer to an 11x7-in. baking dish coated with cooking spray. Pour sauce over vegetables.
3. Combine bread crumbs and butter; sprinkle over top. Bake, uncovered, at 400° until vegetables are tender and crumbs are golden brown, 15-20 minutes.
Freeze option: Cool unbaked casserole; cover and freeze. To use, partially thaw in refrigerator overnight. Remove from refrigerator 30 minutes before baking. Preheat oven to 375°. Bake casserole as directed, increasing time as necessary to heat through and for a thermometer inserted in center to read 165°.
¾ cup: 189 cal., 7g fat (4g sat. fat), 21mg chol., 309mg sod., 27g carb. (9g sugars, 4g fiber), 7g pro. **Diabetic exchanges:** 1 starch, 1 high-fat meat, 1 vegetable.

SLOW-COOKED RATATOUILLE

I get my son to eat eggplant by cooking low and slow on this classic French veggie dish. A side of rice and garlic cheese bread also help.
—*Diane Goedde, Red Lodge, MT*

PREP: 25 min. + standing • **COOK:** 5 hours
MAKES: 10 servings

- 1 medium eggplant, peeled and cut into 1-in. cubes
- 1 Tbsp. plus 1 tsp. salt, divided
- 2 medium onions, halved and thinly sliced
- 4 medium tomatoes, chopped
- 3 medium zucchini, cut into ¾-in. slices
- 2 celery ribs, chopped
- 3 Tbsp. olive oil
- 2 tsp. dried basil or 2 Tbsp. minced fresh basil
- 4 garlic cloves, minced
- ½ tsp. pepper
- 1 can (6 oz.) tomato paste
- 1 can (2¼ oz.) sliced ripe olives, drained
- ⅓ cup coarsely chopped fresh basil

1. Place eggplant in a colander over a plate; sprinkle with 1 Tbsp. salt and toss. Let stand 45 minutes. Rinse and drain well; blot dry with paper towels.
2. Place eggplant and remaining vegetables in a 5- or 6-qt. slow cooker. Add oil, dried basil, garlic, pepper and remaining 1 tsp. salt; toss to combine.
3. Cook, covered, on low 5-6 hours or until onions are tender. Stir in tomato paste, olives and fresh basil; heat through.
Freeze option: Freeze cooled ratatouille in freezer containers. To use, partially thaw in refrigerator overnight. Microwave, covered, on high in a microwave-safe dish until heated through, stirring gently.
¾ cup: 102 cal., 5g fat (1g sat. fat), 0 chol., 380mg sod., 13g carb. (7g sugars, 4g fiber), 3g pro. **Diabetic exchanges:** 2 vegetable, 1 fat.

DID YOU KNOW?
Ratatouille makes a great side dish for grilled meats as well as chicken breasts baked in the oven or easily prepared on the stovetop. Many enjoy it as a meatless main course alongside garlic bread and salad.

OVERNIGHT FRUIT SALAD

I first tasted this rich fruit salad at my wedding reception almost 40 years ago. The ladies who did the cooking wouldn't share the recipe at the time, but I eventually got it. I've made it for many meals, and our daughters copied the recipe when they married.
—*Eileen Duffeck, Lena, WI*

- -

PREP: 30 min. + chilling • **MAKES:** 16 servings

- 3 large eggs, beaten
- ¼ cup sugar
- ¼ cup white vinegar
- 2 Tbsp. butter
- 2 cups green grapes
- 2 cups miniature marshmallows
- 1 can (20 oz.) pineapple chunks, drained
- 1 can (15 oz.) mandarin oranges, drained
- 2 medium firm bananas, sliced
- 2 cups heavy whipping cream, whipped
- ½ cup chopped pecans

1. In a double boiler over medium heat, cook and stir eggs, sugar and vinegar until mixture is thickened and reaches 160°. Remove from the heat; stir in butter. Cool.

2. In a large serving bowl, combine grapes, marshmallows, pineapple, oranges and bananas; add cooled dressing and stir to coat. Refrigerate for 4 hours or overnight. Just before serving, fold in whipped cream and pecans.

½ cup: 244 cal., 16g fat (8g sat. fat), 84mg chol., 44mg sod., 24g carb. (21g sugars, 1g fiber), 3g pro.

DIJON VEGGIES WITH COUSCOUS

❄ DIJON VEGGIES WITH COUSCOUS

Coated in a tangy Dijon sauce, these tasty veggies and fluffy couscous make for a delightful side you can make ahead of time.
—*Juliana Dumitru, Fairview Park, OH*

- -

PREP: 20 min. • **BAKE:** 20 min.
MAKES: 6 servings

- ½ lb. medium fresh mushrooms, quartered
- 1 medium zucchini, halved lengthwise and cut into ¼-in. slices
- 1 medium sweet red pepper, cut into 1-in. pieces
- ¼ cup dry red wine or reduced-sodium chicken broth
- 3 Tbsp. Dijon mustard
- 2 Tbsp. olive oil
- 2 garlic cloves, minced
- 1 tsp. prepared horseradish
- ½ tsp. salt
- ¼ tsp. pepper
- 1 cup water
- 1 cup uncooked couscous

1. Place an 18x12-in. piece of heavy-duty foil on a large baking sheet.

2. In a large bowl, combine the mushrooms, zucchini and red pepper. Combine the wine, mustard, oil, garlic, horseradish, salt and pepper; drizzle over vegetables. Toss to coat; transfer to baking sheet. Top with a second large piece of foil. Bring edges of foil pieces together; crimp to seal, forming a large packet.

3. Bake at 350° for 20-25 minutes or until vegetables are tender. Open foil carefully to allow steam to escape.

4. Meanwhile, in a small saucepan, bring water to a boil. Stir in couscous. Remove from the heat; cover and let stand for 5-10 minutes or until water is absorbed. Fluff with a fork. Transfer couscous and vegetables to a large serving bowl; toss to combine.

Freeze option: Freeze cooled couscous mixture in a freezer container. To use, partially thaw in refrigerator overnight. Microwave, covered, on high in a microwave-safe dish until heated through, adding 2-3 Tbsp. water to moisten.

1 serving: 182 cal., 5g fat (1g sat. fat), 0 chol., 388mg sod., 29g carb. (3g sugars, 3g fiber), 6g pro. **Diabetic exchanges:** 1½ starch, 1 vegetable, 1 fat.

MASHED CAULIFLOWER AU GRATIN

Unless someone tells you, you might not even realize that you're eating cauliflower. Even my grandchildren love this buttery, cheesy, creamy dish that tastes like mashed potatoes.
—*Sandie Parker, Elk Rapids, MI*

- -

PREP: 40 min. • **COOK:** 40 min.
MAKES: 12 servings

- 2 **large heads cauliflower, broken into florets**
- 1½ **cups shredded Parmesan cheese**
- 1 **cup shredded Colby-Monterey Jack cheese**
- 6 **Tbsp. butter, cubed**
- ¾ **tsp. garlic salt**
- ½ **tsp. Montreal steak seasoning**

TOPPING

- 1 **cup Italian-style panko bread crumbs**
- ¼ **cup butter, melted**

1. Preheat oven to 350°. Place cauliflower in a stockpot; add water to cover. Bring to a boil. Reduce heat; simmer, uncovered, until very tender, 10-12 minutes. Drain; transfer to a large bowl. Mash cauliflower; stir in cheeses, cubed butter and seasonings. Transfer to a greased 3-qt. or 13x9-in. baking dish.

2. In a small bowl, mix bread crumbs with melted butter until evenly coated; sprinkle over cauliflower mixture. Bake, uncovered, until heated through and topping is golden brown, 40-50 minutes.

Freeze option: Cool unbaked casserole; cover and freeze. To use, partially thaw in refrigerator overnight. Remove from refrigerator 30 minutes before baking. Preheat oven to 350°. Bake casserole as directed, increasing time as necessary to heat through and for a thermometer inserted in center to read 165°.

¾ cup: 238 cal., 17g fat (10g sat. fat), 41mg chol., 612mg sod., 14g carb. (3g sugars, 4g fiber), 9g pro.

Swiss Mashed Cauliflower: Cook and mash cauliflower as directed. Add 1 cup shredded Swiss cheese, 2 Tbsp. butter, 1 tsp. salt, ½ tsp. pepper, ¼ tsp. garlic powder and ¼ to ⅓ cup 2% milk.

BAKED TWO-CHEESE & BACON GRITS

To a Southerner, grits are a true staple. Combine them with some bacon and cheese, and even Northerners will be asking for a second helping.
—*Melissa Rogers, Tuscaloosa, AL*

- -

PREP: 25 min. • **BAKE:** 40 min. + standing
MAKES: 12 servings

- 6 **thick-sliced bacon strips, chopped**
- 3 **cups water**
- 3 **cups chicken stock**
- 1 **tsp. garlic powder**
- ½ **tsp. pepper**
- 2 **cups quick-cooking grits**
- 12 **oz. Velveeta, cubed (about 2⅓ cups)**
- ½ **cup butter, cubed**
- ½ **cup 2% milk**
- 4 **large eggs, room temperature, lightly beaten**
- 2 **cups shredded white cheddar cheese**

1. Preheat oven to 350°. In a large saucepan, cook bacon over medium heat until crisp, stirring occasionally. Remove pan from heat. Remove bacon with a slotted spoon; drain on paper towels.

2. Add water, stock, garlic powder and pepper to bacon drippings; bring to a boil. Slowly stir in grits. Reduce heat to medium-low; cook, covered, 5-7 minutes or until thickened, stirring occasionally. Remove from heat.

3. Add Velveeta and butter; stir until melted. Stir in milk. Slowly stir in eggs until blended. Transfer to a greased 13x9-in. baking dish. Sprinkle with bacon and shredded cheese. Bake, uncovered, 40-45 minutes or until edges are golden brown and cheese is melted. Let stand 10 minutes before serving.

Freeze option: Cool unbaked casserole; cover and freeze. To use, partially thaw in refrigerator overnight. Remove casserole from refrigerator 30 minutes before baking. Bake grits as directed, increasing time to 50-60 minutes or until heated through and a thermometer inserted in center reads 165°.

¾ cup: 466 cal., 34g fat (18g sat. fat), 143mg chol., 840mg sod., 23g carb. (3g sugars, 1g fiber), 17g pro.

MASHED CAULIFLOWER AU GRATIN

JEN'S BAKED BEANS

❄

JEN'S BAKED BEANS

My daughters wanted baked beans, so I gave homemade ones a shot. With mustard, molasses and a dash of heat, I made these beans absolutely delicious.
—*Jennifer Heasley, York, PA*

PREP: 20 min. • **BAKE:** 50 min.
MAKES: 8 servings

6	bacon strips, chopped
4	cans (15½ oz. each) great northern beans, rinsed and drained
1⅓	cups ketchup
⅔	cup packed brown sugar
⅓	cup molasses
3	Tbsp. yellow mustard
2½	tsp. garlic powder
1½	tsp. hot pepper sauce
¼	tsp. crushed red pepper flakes

1. Preheat oven to 325°. In an ovenproof Dutch oven, cook the bacon over medium heat until crisp, stirring occasionally. Remove with a slotted spoon; drain on paper towels. Discard drippings.
2. Return bacon to pan. Stir in remaining ingredients; bring to a boil. Place in oven; bake, covered, 50-60 minutes to allow flavors to blend.

Freeze option: Freeze cooled baked beans in freezer containers. To use, partially thaw in refrigerator overnight. Heat through in a saucepan, stirring occasionally and adding a little broth or water if necessary.

¾ cup: 362 cal., 3g fat (1g sat. fat), 6mg chol., 1000mg sod., 71g carb. (39g sugars, 11g fiber), 13g pro.

TORTELLINI BAKE

❄ TORTELLINI BAKE

Every year I look forward to gardening season. Summer in New Hampshire brings plenty of fresh zucchini and squash. One year I had so much that I was searching for different ways to prepare it, and that's when I came up with this recipe. Serve it as a side dish or on its own as a light meatless meal.
—*Donald Roberts, Amherst, NH*

- -

PREP: 20 min. • **BAKE:** 20 min.
MAKES: 8 servings

1 pkg. (10 oz.) refrigerated cheese tortellini
1 Tbsp. olive oil
1 small zucchini, diced
1 yellow squash, diced
1 onion, diced
1 sweet red pepper, diced
1 tsp. dried basil
½ tsp. pepper
½ tsp. salt
1 cup shredded part-skim mozzarella cheese
1 cup half-and-half cream

1. Cook tortellini according to package directions. Meanwhile, heat oil in a skillet; cook zucchini, yellow squash, onion, red pepper and seasonings until vegetables are crisp-tender.
2. Drain tortellini; combine with vegetable mixture, mozzarella and cream in a 1½-qt. baking dish.
3. Bake, uncovered, at 375° until heated through, about 20 minutes.
Freeze option: Cool unbaked casserole; cover and freeze. To use, partially thaw in refrigerator overnight. Remove from refrigerator 30 minutes before baking. Preheat oven to 375°. Bake casserole as directed, increasing time as necessary to heat through and for a thermometer inserted in center to read 165°.
¾ cup: 219 cal., 10g fat (5g sat. fat), 38mg chol., 362mg sod., 22g carb. (5g sugars, 2g fiber), 10g pro.

MAKE-AHEAD HEARTY SIX-LAYER SALAD

This salad is an all-time favorite. I reach for the recipe whenever I need a dish to pass. It's easy to make, can be assembled ahead of time and looks great.
—*Noreen Meyer, Madison, WI*

- -

PREP: 20 min. + chilling • **MAKES:** 12 servings

- 1½ **cups uncooked small pasta shells**
- 1 **Tbsp. vegetable oil**
- 3 **cups shredded lettuce**
- 3 **large hard-boiled large eggs, sliced**
- ¼ **tsp. salt**
- ⅛ **tsp. pepper**
- 2 **cups shredded cooked chicken breast**
- 1 **pkg. (10 oz.) frozen peas, thawed**

DRESSING
- 1 **cup mayonnaise**
- ¼ **cup sour cream**
- 2 **green onions, chopped**
- 2 **tsp. Dijon mustard**

TOPPINGS
- 1 **cup shredded Colby or Monterey Jack cheese**
- 2 **Tbsp. minced fresh parsley**

1. Cook pasta according to package directions; drain and rinse with cold water. Drizzle with oil and toss to coat.

2. Place the lettuce in a 2½-qt. glass serving bowl; top with pasta and eggs. Sprinkle with salt and pepper. Layer with chicken and peas. In a small bowl, mix dressing ingredients until blended; spread over top. Refrigerate, covered, for several hours or overnight.

3. Just before serving, sprinkle with cheese and parsley.

¾ cup: 310 cal., 22g fat (5g sat. fat), 84mg chol., 287mg sod., 13g carb. (2g sugars, 2g fiber), 14g pro.

TEST KITCHEN TIPS
Layer in other greens for the lettuce if you prefer. Baby spinach and peppery arugula are great choices. Lighten things up by using low-fat sour cream and low-fat mayonnaise.

MAKE-AHEAD CREAMY FRUIT SALAD

We love fruit salads for our holiday dinners. I experimented and came up with this delicious medley—it reminds us of the tropics in the middle of winter! I sometimes add sliced bananas just before serving. Feel free to use your own favorite fruits.
—*Joan Hallford, North Richland Hills, TX*

- -

PREP: 20 min. + chilling • **MAKES:** 6 cups

- ¾ **cup pina colada yogurt**
- ¾ **cup Key lime yogurt**
- ½ **cup heavy whipping cream, whipped**
- 1 **Tbsp. Key lime juice**
- 2 **cups mandarin oranges, drained**
- 1 **can (15 oz.) peach halves in light syrup, drained and sliced**
- 1 **cup miniature marshmallows**
- 1 **cup unsweetened crushed pineapple, drained**
- ½ **cup sweetened shredded coconut**
- ½ **cup pitted dark sweet cherries, drained and halved**
- ¼ **cup chopped pecans, toasted**

In a large bowl, combine the yogurts, whipped cream and lime juice. Gently fold in remaining ingredients. Refrigerate, covered, until serving.
¾ cup: 250 cal., 11g fat (6g sat. fat), 19mg chol., 56mg sod., 38g carb. (35g sugars, 2g fiber), 4g pro.

MAKE-AHEAD HEARTY SIX-LAYER SALAD

CRANBERRY CORNBREAD CASSEROLE

❄ PECAN RICE PILAF

This is one of my stand-by side dishes, which can complement most meat and meatless entrees. It is special enough for company and quick enough for weeknights.
—*Jacqueline Oglesby, Spruce Pine, NC*

- -

PREP: 15 min. • **COOK:** 20 min.
MAKES: 9 servings

- 1 cup chopped pecans
- 5 Tbsp. butter, divided
- 1 small onion, chopped
- 2 cups uncooked long grain rice
- 1 carton (32 oz.) chicken broth
- 3 Tbsp. minced fresh parsley, divided
- ½ tsp. salt
- ¼ tsp. dried thyme
- ⅛ tsp. pepper
- 1 cup shredded carrots

1. In a large saucepan, saute pecans in 2 Tbsp. butter until toasted; remove from the pan and set aside.
2. In the same pan, saute onion in remaining butter until tender. Add rice; cook and stir until rice is lightly browned, 3-4 minutes. Stir in the broth, 2 Tbsp. parsley, salt, thyme and pepper. Bring to a boil. Reduce heat; cover and simmer for 10 minutes.
3. Add carrots; simmer until rice is tender, 3-5 minutes longer. Stir in toasted pecans and remaining parsley. Fluff with a fork.

Freeze option: Reserving pecans for later, freeze cooled pilaf in a freezer container. To use, partially thaw in refrigerator overnight. Microwave, covered, on high in a microwave-safe dish, adding 2-3 Tbsp. water to moisten, until heated through. Toast pecans; add to the pilaf.

¾ cup: 313 cal., 16g fat (5g sat. fat), 19mg chol., 623mg sod., 37g carb. (2g sugars, 2g fiber), 5g pro.

❄ CRANBERRY CORNBREAD CASSEROLE

What could be better on a cold day than a warm casserole and creamy sweet cornbread put together? Because it starts with a mix, this side takes no time to make. Just bake, scoop and eat. Yum!
—*Valery Anderson, Sterling Heights, MI*

- -

PREP: 15 min. • **BAKE:** 20 min.
MAKES: 9 servings

- ½ cup dried cranberries
- ½ cup boiling water
- 1 pkg. (8½ oz.) cornbread/muffin mix
- 1 tsp. onion powder
- ¼ tsp. rubbed sage
- 1 large egg
- 1 can (14¾ oz.) cream-style corn
- 2 Tbsp. butter, melted
- ¼ cup chopped pecans
- ½ tsp. grated orange zest

1. Place cranberries in a small bowl; cover with boiling water. Let stand for 5 minutes; drain.
2. In a small bowl, combine the muffin mix, onion powder and sage. In another bowl, whisk the egg, corn and butter; stir into dry ingredients just until moistened. Fold in the pecans, orange zest and cranberries.
3. Transfer to a greased 8-in. square baking dish. Bake uncovered at 400° for 20-25 minutes or until set.

Freeze option: Cool baked cornbread in pan; cover and freeze. To use, partially thaw in refrigerator overnight. Remove from refrigerator 30 minutes before baking. Preheat oven to 350°. Reheat cornbread 10-12 minutes or until heated through.

1 piece: 225 cal., 9g fat (3g sat. fat), 28mg chol., 369mg sod., 35g carb. (14g sugars, 3g fiber), 4g pro. **Diabetic exchanges:** 2 starch, 1 fat.

MINI SWEET POTATO
SCONES WITH ROSEMARY
& BACON, P. 101

Make-Ahead Breads

Hooray for hot homemade bread!
Get fresh-baked flavor on any schedule.

SLOW-COOKER
PUMPKIN YEAST BREAD, P. 99

EASY PEASY BISCUITS

I can make these biscuits and have enough left over to freeze for another meal. They are wonderful with homemade peach preserves.

—Amanda West, Shelbyville, TN

PREP: 25 min. • **BAKE:** 10 min.
MAKES: 2 dozen

4	cups all-purpose flour
4	Tbsp. baking powder
1	Tbsp. sugar
1	Tbsp. ground flaxseed
1	tsp. sea salt
1	cup solid coconut oil
1½	cups 2% milk

1. Preheat oven to 450°. In a large bowl, whisk flour, baking powder, sugar, flaxseed and salt. Add coconut oil and cut in with a pastry blender until mixture resembles coarse crumbs. Add milk; stir just until moistened.

2. Turn onto a lightly floured surface; knead gently 8-10 times. Pat or roll dough into a rectangle ½ in. thick; fold dough into thirds (as you would a letter). Pat or roll dough again into a rectangle ½ in. thick; cut with a pizza cutter or knife into 24 biscuits, each about 2½ in. square. Place 1½ in. apart on ungreased baking sheets. Bake until biscuits are light brown, 8-10 minutes. Serve warm.

Freeze option: Freeze cut biscuit dough on waxed paper-lined baking sheets until firm. Transfer to airtight containers; return to freezer. To use, bake biscuits in a preheated 350° oven until light brown, 15-20 minutes.

1 biscuit: 167 cal., 10g fat (8g sat. fat), 1mg chol., 328mg sod., 17g carb. (1g sugars, 1g fiber), 3g pro.

OVERNIGHT CHERRY DANISH

OVERNIGHT CHERRY DANISH

These rolls with their cherry-filled centers melt in your mouth. They store well, unfrosted, in the freezer.

—Leann Sauder, Tremont, IL

PREP: 1½ hours + chilling • **BAKE:** 15 min.
MAKES: 3 dozen

2	pkg. (¼ oz. each) active dry yeast
½	cup warm 2% milk (110° to 115°)
6	cups all-purpose flour
⅓	cup sugar
2	tsp. salt
1	cup cold butter, cubed
1½	cups warm half-and-half cream (70° to 80°)
6	large egg yolks, room temperature
1	can (21 oz.) cherry pie filling

ICING

3	cups confectioners' sugar
2	Tbsp. butter, softened
¼	tsp. vanilla extract
	Dash salt
4	to 5 Tbsp. half-and-half cream

1. In a small bowl, dissolve yeast in warm milk. In a large bowl, combine flour, sugar and salt. Cut in butter until crumbly. Add yeast mixture, cream and egg yolks; stir until mixture forms a soft dough (dough will be sticky). Refrigerate, covered, overnight.

2. Punch down dough. Turn onto a lightly floured surface; divide into 4 portions. Roll each portion into an 18x4-in. rectangle; cut into 4x1-in. strips.

3. Place 2 strips side by side; twist together. Shape into a ring and pinch ends together. Place 2 in. apart on greased baking sheets. Repeat with remaining strips. Cover with kitchen towels; let rise in a warm place until doubled, about 45 minutes.

4. Preheat oven to 350°. Using the end of a wooden spoon handle, make a ½-in.-deep indentation in the center of each Danish. Fill each with about 1 Tbsp. pie filling. Bake until lightly browned, 14-16 minutes. Remove from pans to wire racks to cool.

5. For icing, in a bowl, beat confectioners' sugar, butter, vanilla, salt and enough cream to reach desired consistency. Drizzle on pastries.

1 pastry: 218 cal., 8g fat (5g sat. fat), 55mg chol., 188mg sod., 33g carb. (16g sugars, 1g fiber), 3g pro.

SLOW-COOKER BANANA BREAD

I love using my slow cooker. I even started to experiment with making bread in it; that way I wouldn't have to heat up my kitchen by turning on my oven. It's so simple. I now make it this way all the time.
—Nicole Gackowski, Antioch, CA

PREP: 10 min. • **COOK:** 2½ hours
MAKES: 16 servings

- 5 medium ripe bananas
- 2½ cups self-rising flour
- 1 can (14 oz.) sweetened condensed milk
- 1 tsp. ground cinnamon
  Cinnamon sugar, optional

1. Place a piece of parchment into a 5-qt. slow cooker, letting ends extend up sides. Grease paper with cooking spray. Combine the first 4 ingredients in a large bowl. Pour batter into prepared slow cooker. If desired, sprinkle cinnamon sugar over the top of batter. Cover slow cooker with a double layer of white paper towels; place lid securely over towels.
2. Cook, covered, on high until bread is lightly browned, 2½-3 hours. To avoid scorching, rotate slow cooker insert a half turn midway through cooking, lifting carefully with oven mitts. Remove bread from slow cooker using parchment to lift; cool slightly before slicing.
Note: As a substitute for each 1 cup of self-rising flour, place 1½ tsp. baking powder and ½ tsp. salt in a measuring cup. Add all-purpose flour to measure 1 cup.
1 piece: 210 cal., 3g fat (2g sat. fat), 11mg chol., 276mg sod., 41g carb. (23g sugars, 2g fiber), 5g pro.

SLOW-COOKER BANANA BREAD

GARLIC PARMESAN BREAD

This is one of my favorite breads. It tastes amazing with everything from bologna sandwiches to spaghetti. And it smells so delicious while it's baking!
—Jami Blunt, Hardy, AR

PREP: 10 min. • **BAKE:** 3 hours
MAKES: 1 loaf (16 pieces)

- 1 cup water (70° to 80°)
- 2 Tbsp. plus 1½ tsp. butter, softened
- 1 Tbsp. honey
- ⅔ cup grated Parmesan cheese
- 1½ tsp. garlic powder
- ¾ tsp. salt
- 3 cups bread flour
- 2¼ tsp. active dry yeast

In bread machine pan, place all ingredients in order suggested by manufacturer. Select basic bread setting. Choose crust color and loaf size if available. Bake according to bread machine directions (after 5 minutes of mixing, check dough and add 1-2 Tbsp. of water or flour if needed).
Freeze option: Securely wrap cooled loaf in foil and then freeze. To use, thaw loaf at room temperature.
1 piece: 112 cal., 3g fat (2g sat. fat), 7mg chol., 191mg sod., 18g carb. (1g sugars, 1g fiber), 5g pro.

PEACHES & CREAM
WHISKEY LOAF

PEACHES & CREAM WHISKEY LOAF

I love when fresh peaches are in season! This recipe is sweet from the peaches and has a slight tang from the whiskey. It's perfect as an after-dinner sweet, and it's just as good with morning coffee. It also makes a wonderful gift for neighbors and friends.
—*Anne Ormond, Dover, NH*

- -

PREP: 20 min. • **BAKE:** 1 hour + cooling
MAKES: 1 loaf (12 pieces)

- 1½   **cups all-purpose flour**
- 1   **cup packed brown sugar**
- 1¼   **tsp. baking soda**
- 2   **large eggs, room temperature**
- ⅓   **cup sour cream**
- ¼   **cup canola oil**
- 2   **Tbsp. peach whiskey or whiskey**
- 1   **cup chopped peeled fresh peaches**
- ½   **cup chopped pecans**

GLAZE

- 1   **cup confectioners' sugar**
- 1   **to 2 Tbsp. 2% milk**
- 1   **Tbsp. peach whiskey or whiskey**

1. Preheat oven to 350°. In a large bowl, whisk flour, brown sugar and baking soda. In another bowl, whisk eggs, sour cream, oil and whiskey until blended. Add to flour mixture; stir just until moistened. Fold in peaches and pecans.
2. Transfer to a greased 8x4-in. loaf pan. Bake until a toothpick inserted into center comes out clean, about 1 hour. Cool 10 minutes in pan before removing to a wire rack to cool completely. Combine the glaze ingredients; drizzle over cooled bread. Let stand until set.
Freeze option: Securely wrap cooled loaf in foil and then freeze. To use, thaw loaf at room temperature.
1 piece: 273 cal., 10g fat (2g sat. fat), 33mg chol., 151mg sod., 42g carb. (29g sugars, 1g fiber), 3g pro.

READER REVIEW
"Delicious ! I only made a half-recipe of the glaze."

MARTHA146, TASTEOFHOME.COM

APRICOT-ROSEMARY SCONES

APRICOT-ROSEMARY SCONES

Turn these sweet-savory scones into a family baking project. Making them is a delightful way to show your love on Mother's Day.
—*Charlene Chambers, Ormond Beach, FL*

- -

PREP: 25 min. • **BAKE:** 15 min.
MAKES: 16 scones

- 4   **cups all-purpose flour**
- 2   **Tbsp. sugar**
- 2   **Tbsp. baking powder**
- ¾   **tsp. salt**
- 1½   **cups cold butter, cubed**
- 1   **cup chopped dried apricots**
- 1   **Tbsp. minced fresh rosemary**
- 4   **large eggs, room temperature, lightly beaten**
- 1   **cup cold heavy whipping cream**

TOPPING

- 1   **large egg, lightly beaten**
- 2   **Tbsp. 2% milk**
- 2   **tsp. sugar**

1. Preheat oven to 400°. Whisk together flour, sugar, baking powder and salt. Cut in cold butter to the size of peas. Stir in apricots and rosemary.
2. In a separate bowl, whisk the eggs and whipping cream until blended. Stir into flour-butter mixture just until moistened.
3. Turn dough onto a well-floured surface; roll into a 10-in. square. Cut into 4 squares; cut each square into 4 triangles. Place on baking sheets lined with parchment.
4. For topping, combine egg and milk. Brush tops of scones with egg mixture; sprinkle with sugar. Bake until golden brown, 12-15 minutes.
Freeze option: Freeze cooled scones in resealable freezer containers. To use, reheat in a preheated 350° oven 20-25 minutes, adding time as necessary to heat through.
1 scone: 372 cal., 25g fat (15g sat. fat), 121mg chol., 461mg sod., 32g carb. (7g sugars, 1g fiber), 6g pro.

OVERNIGHT ROLLS

I've made these light, tender rolls for 25 years. I once served them to a woman who'd been in the restaurant business for half a century. She said they were the best rolls she'd ever tasted.
—*Dorothy Yagodich, Charlerio, PA*

PREP: 25 min. + chilling • **BAKE:** 15 min.
MAKES: 20 rolls

- 1 pkg. (¼ oz.) active dry yeast
- ½ cup plus ¾ tsp. sugar, divided
- 1⅓ cups plus 3 Tbsp. warm water (110° to 115°), divided
- ⅓ cup canola oil
- 1 large egg, room temperature
- 1 tsp. salt
- 4¾ to 5¼ cups all-purpose flour
  Melted butter, optional

1. In a bowl, dissolve yeast and ¾ tsp. sugar in 3 Tbsp. warm water. Add remaining ½ cup sugar, remaining 3⅓ cups water, oil, egg, salt and 2 cups flour; mix well. Add enough remaining flour to form a soft dough.
2. Turn onto a floured surface; knead until smooth and elastic, 6-8 minutes. Place in a greased bowl, turning once to grease top. Cover and let rise in a warm place until doubled, about 1 hour.
3. Punch dough down. Shape into 20 balls. Roll each into an 8-in. rope; tie into a loose knot. Place on a greased baking sheet; cover and refrigerate overnight. Allow rolls to sit at room temperature 45 minutes before baking.
4. Bake at 375° for 12-15 minutes or until lightly browned. Brush with butter if desired. Remove to wire racks to cool.
1 roll: 165 cal., 4g fat (1g sat. fat), 11mg chol., 122mg sod., 28g carb. (6g sugars, 1g fiber), 4g pro.

❄ CHERRY-CHIP OAT SCONES

My family loves scones and anything with oatmeal. I started with my basic scone recipe and added oat flour to increase the oat taste and texture, as well as ingredients that are harmonious with the mellow taste of oats. I have learned that everyone loves them most when I add special ingredients you can find in each bite.
—*Amy Brnger, Portsmouth, NH*

PREP: 15 min. • **BAKE:** 20 min.
MAKES: 10 scones

- 1½ cups all-purpose flour
- ½ cup oat flour
- ½ cup old-fashioned oats
- 3 Tbsp. brown sugar
- 1 tsp. baking soda
- 1 tsp. cream of tartar
- ½ tsp. salt
- 3 Tbsp. cold butter, cubed
- 1 cup buttermilk
- ⅓ cup dried cherries, chopped
- ⅓ cup miniature semisweet chocolate chips
- ¼ cup finely chopped pecans, toasted

TOPPING
- 1 Tbsp. coarse sugar
- 1 Tbsp. old-fashioned oats

1. Preheat oven to 400°. Whisk together first 7 ingredients; cut in butter until mixture resembles coarse crumbs. Add buttermilk, stirring just until moistened. Stir in cherries, chocolate chips and pecans.
2. Transfer to a parchment-lined baking sheet; pat dough into a 6-in. circle. Cut dough circle into 10 wedges, but do not separate them. Sprinkle with coarse sugar and oats.
3. Bake until golden brown, 20-25 minutes. Serve warm.

Freeze option: Freeze cooled scones in freezer containers. To use, thaw at room temperature or, if desired, microwave each scone on high until heated through, 20-30 seconds.
1 scone: 229 cal., 8g fat (4g sat. fat), 10mg chol., 321mg sod., 36g carb. (13g sugars, 2g fiber), 5g pro.

CHERRY-CHIP OAT SCONES

SLOW-COOKER
PUMPKIN YEAST BREAD

BEERNANA BREAD

It's simple arithmetic: Beer is good. Banana bread is good. Beernana bread is great! The recipe is a guaranteed crowd-pleaser. Even novices who don't know their way around the kitchen can pull this one off.
—*Steve Cayford, Dubuque, IA*

- -

PREP: 15 min. • **BAKE:** 55 min. + cooling
MAKES: 1 loaf (16 slices)

- 3 cups self-rising flour
- ¾ cup quick-cooking oats
- ½ cup packed brown sugar
- 1½ cups mashed ripe bananas (about 3 medium)
- 1 bottle (12 oz.) wheat beer
- ¼ cup maple syrup
- 2 Tbsp. olive oil
- 1 Tbsp. sesame seeds
- ¼ tsp. kosher salt

1. Preheat oven to 375°. In a large bowl, mix flour, oats and brown sugar. In another bowl, mix bananas, beer and maple syrup until blended. Add banana mixture to flour mixture; stir just until moistened.

2. Transfer to a greased 9x5-in. loaf pan. Drizzle with oil; sprinkle with sesame seeds and salt. Bake until a toothpick inserted in center comes out clean, 55-60 minutes. Cool in pan 10 minutes before removing to wire rack to cool.

Freeze option: Securely wrap cooled loaf in foil and then freeze. To use, thaw bread at room temperature.

1 piece: 173 cal., 2g fat (0 sat. fat), 0 chol., 304mg sod., 35g carb. (13g sugars, 1g fiber), 3g pro. **Diabetic exchanges:** 2 starch, ½ fat.

SLOW-COOKER PUMPKIN YEAST BREAD

Savor the rich flavors of fall with this homey loaf you can bake up in the slow cooker. Butterscotch adds a sweet surprise.
—*Erica Polly, Sun Prairie, WI*

- -

PREP: 20 min. • **COOK:** 2½ hours + cooling
MAKES: 1 loaf (12 pieces)

- ⅓ cup packed brown sugar
- 1 pkg. (¼ oz.) quick-rise yeast
- 2 tsp. pumpkin pie spice
- ¾ tsp. salt
- 3½ to 4 cups all-purpose flour
- ¾ cup 2% milk
- 2 Tbsp. butter, cubed
- ¾ cup canned pumpkin
- 1 large egg, room temperature, lightly beaten
- ⅓ cup raisins
- ⅓ cup chopped pecans, toasted
- ⅓ cup butterscotch chips, optional

1. In a large bowl, mix brown sugar, yeast, pie spice, salt and 1½ cups flour. In a small saucepan, heat milk and butter to 120°-130°; stir into dry ingredients. Stir in pumpkin, egg and enough remaining flour to form a soft dough (dough will be sticky).

2. Turn dough onto a floured surface; knead until smooth and elastic, 6-8 minutes. During the last few minutes of kneading add raisins, pecans and, if desired, butterscotch chips. Shape into a 6-in. round loaf; transfer to a greased double thickness of heavy-duty foil (about 12 in. square). Lifting with foil, place in a 6-qt. slow cooker. Press foil against bottom and sides of slow cooker.

3. Cook, covered, on high 2½-3 hours or until a thermometer reads 190°-200°. Remove to a wire rack and cool completely before slicing.

1 piece: 228 cal., 5g fat (2g sat. fat), 22mg chol., 180mg sod., 40g carb. (10g sugars, 2g fiber), 6g pro.

❄ EASY BATTER ROLLS

The first thing my guests ask when they come for dinner is if I'm serving these dinner rolls. The buns are so light, airy and delicious that I'm regularly asked for the recipe.
—*Thomasina Brunner, Gloversville, NY*

PREP: 30 min. + rising • **BAKE:** 15 min.
MAKES: 1 dozen

- 3 cups all-purpose flour
- 2 Tbsp. sugar
- 1 pkg. (¼ oz.) active dry yeast
- 1 tsp. salt
- 1 cup water
- 2 Tbsp. butter
- 1 large egg, room temperature
  Melted butter

1. In a large mixing bowl, combine 2 cups flour, sugar, yeast and salt. In a saucepan, heat the water and butter to 120°-130°. Add to the dry ingredients; beat until blended. Add egg; beat on low speed for 30 seconds, then on high for 3 minutes. Stir in enough of the remaining flour to form a stiff dough. Do not knead. Cover and let dough rise in a warm place until doubled, about 30 minutes.

2. Stir dough down. Fill 12 greased muffin cups half full. Cover and let rise until doubled, about 15 minutes.

3. Bake at 350° 15-20 minutes or until golden brown. Cool for 1 minute; remove from pan to a wire rack. Brush tops with melted butter.

Freeze option: Freeze cooled rolls in airtight containers. To use, microwave each roll on high until warmed, 30-45 seconds.

1 roll: 147 cal., 3g fat (1g sat. fat), 21mg chol., 219mg sod., 26g carb. (2g sugars, 1g fiber), 4g pro.

DID YOU KNOW?

Batter bread lets you simply enjoy homemade yeast bread without the work of kneading. It dirties fewer dishes, and it leaves your counter clean, since the dough stays in its mixing bowl for the first rise. Since beating the batter with a mixer takes the place of kneading, be sure to beat for the time specified in the recipe. Batter bread dough is more loose and sticky than a traditional kneaded dough.

EASY BATTER ROLLS

MINI SWEET POTATO
SCONES WITH ROSEMARY
& BACON

MINI SWEET POTATO SCONES WITH ROSEMARY & BACON

I grow my own sweet potatoes, so I'm always thinking of new ways to use them. I created this recipe on a whim and am thrilled with the results—everyone who tries these scones loves them. To save a little time in the morning, I like to combine the dry ingredients and cut in the butter the night before. I usually stir in the crumbled bacon at that time too. Cover and refrigerate overnight, then proceed with the recipe the next morning. In addition to saving time, this also allows the rosemary and bacon flavors to permeate. Chilling the butter (in the mix) results in very tender scones.
—Sue Gronholz, Beaver Dam, WI

PREP: 30 min. • **BAKE:** 15 min.
MAKES: 16 scones

2½ cups all-purpose flour
½ cup sugar
2½ tsp. baking powder
1½ tsp. pumpkin pie spice or
    ground cinnamon
1½ tsp. minced fresh rosemary or
    ½ tsp. dried rosemary, crushed
½ tsp. salt
¼ tsp. baking soda
½ cup cold butter
4 bacon strips, cooked and crumbled
½ cup mashed sweet potatoes
¼ cup plain Greek yogurt
1 large egg, room temperature
2 Tbsp. maple syrup
TOPPING
1 Tbsp. 2% milk
1 Tbsp. sugar

1. Preheat oven to 425°. In a large bowl, whisk the first 7 ingredients. Cut in the butter until the mixture resembles coarse crumbs. Stir in bacon. In another bowl, whisk sweet potatoes, yogurt, egg and maple syrup until blended; stir into crumb mixture just until combined.
2. Turn onto a floured surface; knead gently 10 times. Divide dough in half. Pat each half into a 6-in. circle. Cut each into 8 wedges. Place wedges on a greased baking sheet. Brush with milk; sprinkle with sugar. Bake until golden brown, 12-14 minutes. Serve warm.
Freeze option: Freeze cooled scones in airtight freezer containers. To use, thaw before serving or, if desired, reheat on a baking sheet in a preheated 350° oven until warmed, 3-4 minutes.
1 scone: 184 cal., 7g fat (4g sat. fat), 30mg chol., 261mg sod., 26g carb. (9g sugars, 1g fiber), 3g pro.

RUSTIC HONEY CAKE, P. 108

Timesaving Desserts

Beating the clock doesn't mean skipping dessert! Check out these sweet treats that offer plan-ahead ease.

FRIED ICE CREAM DESSERT BARS, P. 106

COFFEE ICE CREAM COOKIE CUPS

I'm 11 years old with six brothers and sisters, and we're always looking for new ice cream recipes. I invented this for my sister's birthday party, and everyone complimented it and wanted more. I've also tried it with peanut butter cookie dough and different flavored ice creams, but I like this combination the best.
—*Marcus Dooley, Red Oak, TX*

- -

PREP: 30 min. • **BAKE:** 15 min. + freezing
MAKES: 1 dozen

- 1   tube (16½ oz.) refrigerated chocolate chip cookie dough
- 2   cups coffee ice cream
     Whipped cream and chocolate syrup
- ⅓   cup English toffee bits or almond brickle chips

1. Preheat oven to 350°. Let dough stand at room temperature 5-10 minutes to soften. Cut into 12 slices; press onto bottoms and up the sides of greased muffin cups.

2. Bake until golden brown, 12-14 minutes. Cool slightly on a wire rack. Spoon ice cream into each cup. Cover and freeze until firm, 1-2 hours.

3. Remove cookie cups from pan. Garnish with whipped cream and chocolate syrup. Sprinkle with toffee bits.

1 ice cream cookie cup: 255 cal., 13g fat (5g sat. fat), 20mg chol., 131mg sod., 33g carb. (24g sugars, 1g fiber), 2g pro.

❄ WHITE CHOCOLATE CRANBERRY-ORANGE BARS

Our family is scattered across the country now. Making a recipe inspired by my mom reminds me of home. No pastry cutter? Just use two sharp knives.
—*Erin Powell, Amarillo, TX*

- -

PREP: 10 min. • **BAKE:** 30 min. + cooling
MAKES: 2 dozen

- 1½   cups all-purpose flour
- ½   cup packed brown sugar
- ½   cup cold butter, cubed

FILLING
- 1   large egg, room temperature
- 1   can (14 oz.) sweetened condensed milk
- 1   tsp. grated orange zest
- 1   tsp. orange extract
- 1½   cups white baking chips
- 1   cup dried cranberries

1. Preheat oven to 350°. Line a 13x9-in. pan with foil, letting ends extend up sides; grease foil. In a bowl, mix flour and brown sugar; cut in butter until crumbly. Press onto bottom of prepared pan. Bake until light golden brown, 10-12 minutes. Cool on a wire rack.

2. For filling, whisk together egg, milk, orange zest and extract until blended; stir in baking chips and cranberries. Spread evenly over crust. Bake 20-25 minutes longer or until top is golden brown. Cool 15 minutes in pan on a wire rack. Lifting with the foil, remove bars from pan; gently peel off foil. Cut into bars. Refrigerate leftovers.

Freeze option: Freeze cooled bars in freezer containers, separating layers with waxed paper. To use, thaw before serving.

1 bar: 214 cal., 9g fat (5g sat. fat), 26mg chol., 66mg sod., 31g carb. (25g sugars, 1g fiber), 3g pro.

WHITE CHOCOLATE CRANBERRY-ORANGE BARS

LEMON COCONUT
STREUSEL
ICE CREAM CAKE

FROSTY GINGER PUMPKIN SQUARES

My family loves getting together to sample good food. While pumpkin makes it perfect for the holidays, this dessert is requested all year.
—*Kathryn Reeger, Shelocta, PA*

PREP: 30 min. + freezing • **MAKES:** 15 servings

- ¼ cup butter, melted
- 1 cup crushed graham cracker (about 16 squares)
- 1 cup crushed gingersnaps (about 18 cookies)
- 2 cups canned pumpkin
- 1 cup sugar
- ½ to 1 tsp. ground cinnamon
- ½ tsp. salt
- ½ tsp. ground ginger
- ¼ tsp. ground nutmeg
- 1 cup chopped walnuts
- ½ gallon vanilla ice cream, slightly softened

1. In a large bowl, combine the butter, graham crackers and gingersnaps. Press two-thirds of the crumb mixture into an ungreased 13x9-in. baking pan.
2. In a large bowl, combine the pumpkin, sugar, cinnamon, salt, ginger and nutmeg. Stir in walnuts. Fold in softened ice cream. Spoon into crust. Sprinkle remaining crumb mixture over top. Freeze until firm, about 3 hours.
1 piece: 351 cal., 18g fat (8g sat. fat), 39mg chol., 234mg sod., 46g carb. (33g sugars, 2g fiber), 5g pro.

❄

LEMON COCONUT STREUSEL ICE CREAM CAKE

I developed this cool treat because I wanted to find a new use for cream of coconut. My family loves this dessert anytime, but especially on a hot summer day. The sweet coconut combines beautifully with the tart lemon juice, and the streusel adds a nice crunch. Look for cream of coconut in the cocktail mixer section of your grocery store. Substitute any crunchy sugar, lemon or coconut cookie you'd like.
—*Janet Gill, Canton, OH*

PREP: 30 min. + freezing • **MAKES:** 16 servings

- 1 pkg. (11.2 oz.) shortbread cookies
- ½ cup sweetened shredded coconut, toasted
- ¼ cup macadamia nuts, coarsely chopped and toasted
- 1 tsp. grated lemon zest
- 1 can (15 oz.) cream of coconut
- ½ cup lemon juice
- 1½ qt. vanilla ice cream, softened
- 1 carton (8 oz.) frozen whipped topping, thawed, divided
  Optional: Fresh blueberries, raspberries and strawberries

1. Reserve 10 cookies for decoration. Crush remaining cookies; transfer to a bowl. Stir in coconut, macadamia nuts and lemon zest. Reserve 2 Tbsp. crumb mixture for topping. In a large bowl, whisk cream of coconut and lemon juice until combined. Stir in softened vanilla ice cream until smooth. Fold in 1 cup whipped topping.
2. Sprinkle 1 cup crumb mixture onto bottom of a greased 9-in. springform pan. Top with half the ice cream mixture. Layer with the remaining 1 cup crumbs and remaining ice cream mixture. Place reserved whole cookies around edge of pan. Top with the remaining 2½ cups whipped topping; sprinkle with reserved 2 Tbsp. crumb mixture. Freeze, covered, until firm, at least 8 hours or overnight. If desired, serve with berries.
Note: To toast nuts and coconut, bake them in separate shallow pans in a 350° oven for 5-10 minutes or until golden brown, stirring them occasionally.
1 piece: 384 cal., 21g fat (13g sat. fat), 29mg chol., 149mg sod., 45g carb. (35g sugars, 1g fiber), 4g pro.

PECAN PUMPKIN
PIE PINWHEELS

FRIED ICE CREAM DESSERT BARS

Fried ice cream is such a delicious treat, but it can be a hassle to make the individual servings. This recipe gives you the same fabulous flavor in an easy and convenient bar form.
—*Andrea Price, Grafton, WI*

PREP: 25 min. + freezing
COOK: 5 min. + cooling
MAKES: 16 servings

- ½ cup butter, cubed
- 2 cups crushed cornflakes
- 1½ tsp. ground cinnamon
- 3 Tbsp. sugar
- 1¾ cups heavy whipping cream
- ¼ cup evaporated milk
- ⅛ tsp. salt
- 1 can (14 oz.) sweetened condensed milk
- 2 tsp. vanilla extract
  Optional: Honey, whipped cream and maraschino cherries

1. In a large skillet, melt butter over medium heat. Add the cornflakes and cinnamon; cook and stir until golden brown, about 5 minutes. Remove mixture from heat; stir in sugar. Let cool completely.
2. In a large bowl, beat cream, evaporated milk and salt until mixture begins to thicken. Gradually beat in condensed milk and vanilla until thickened.
3. Sprinkle half the cornflakes onto bottom of a greased 9-in. square baking pan. Pour creamy filling over crust, then sprinkle with remaining cornflakes. Cover; freeze overnight. Cut into bars. If desired, serve with honey, whipped cream and cherries.
1 bar: 276 cal., 18g fat (11g sat. fat), 55mg chol., 187mg sod., 27g carb. (18g sugars, 0 fiber), 4g pro.

❄ PECAN PUMPKIN PIE PINWHEELS

These pie-like cookie spirals are a pretty way to bring pumpkin flavor to dessert.
—*Kathy Yarosh, Apopka, FL*

PREP: 45 min. + chilling
BAKE: 20 min./batch + cooling
MAKES: 4 dozen

- 1½ cups solid-pack pumpkin
- ½ cup sweetened shredded coconut
- ½ cup finely chopped pecans
- ¼ cup packed brown sugar
- 1 tsp. ground cinnamon
- 1 tsp. pumpkin pie spice
- 1 pkg. (11 oz.) pie crust mix
- ½ cup cream cheese frosting
- 1 to 2 tsp. 2% milk

1. Combine the first 6 ingredients in a small bowl. Prepare pie crust mix according to package directions; divide dough in half.
2. Roll each portion into a 14x8-in. rectangle on lightly floured pieces of waxed paper.

Spread half of pumpkin mixture over 1 dough rectangle to within ¼ in. of edges. Roll up tightly jelly-roll style, starting with a long side. Wrap in waxed paper. Repeat with remaining dough. Freeze 30 minutes or until firm.
3. Preheat oven to 400°. Using a sharp serrated knife, trim ends and cut dough crosswise into ¼-in. slices. Place 1 in. apart on parchment-lined baking sheets. Bake 18-22 minutes or until light golden. Remove from pans to wire racks; cool completely.
4. In a small bowl, combine frosting and enough milk to reach a drizzling consistency. Drizzle over pinwheels; let stand until set. Store between pieces of waxed paper in airtight containers.
Freeze option: Place wrapped logs in an airtight freezer container; return to freezer. To use, unwrap frozen logs and cut into slices. If necessary, let dough stand 15 minutes at room temperature before cutting. Bake as directed, increasing time by 2-4 minutes.
1 cookie: 67 cal., 4g fat (2g sat. fat), 0 chol., 55mg sod., 7g carb. (3g sugars, 0 fiber), 1g pro.

FRIED ICE CREAM
DESSERT BARS

STRAWBERRY CRUNCH ICE CREAM CAKE

Growing up, I loved treats from the ice cream truck that rolled through my neighborhood. This ice cream cake is inspired by one of those crunchy strawberry novelties.

—Lisa Kaminski, Wauwatosa, WI

- -

PREP: 20 min. + freezing
BAKE: 25 min. + cooling • **MAKES:** 9 servings

- 36   Golden Oreo cookies, divided
- 4   Tbsp. butter, melted
- 3   cups vanilla ice cream, softened
- 5   cups strawberry ice cream, softened
- 1   carton (8 oz.) frozen whipped topping, thawed
- 1   pkg. (1 oz.) freeze-dried strawberries, coarsely crushed
     Fresh strawberries, optional

1. Line a 9x9-in. baking pan with parchment. Preheat oven to 350°. Finely crush 24 cookies. In a small bowl, mix cookie crumbs and butter. Press onto bottom of prepared pan. Bake until firm, 25-30 minutes. Cool on a wire rack.
2. Spread vanilla ice cream onto crust; freeze, covered, until firm. Spread with strawberry ice cream and then whipped topping; freeze, covered, until firm.
3. Coarsely crush remaining cookies. Combine cookie crumbs and freeze-dried strawberries; sprinkle over the whipped topping. Freeze, covered, until firm, 8 hours or overnight. Remove from freezer. Lifting with parchment, remove from pan. Gently peel off parchment. Let stand 10 minutes before cutting. If desired, garnish with fresh strawberries.
1 piece: 584 cal., 30g fat (16g sat. fat), 54mg chol., 280mg sod., 72g carb. (33g sugars, 2g fiber), 6g pro.

RUSTIC HONEY CAKE

RUSTIC HONEY CAKE

When my boys were young, they couldn't drink milk but they could have yogurt. This was a cake they could eat. And it's one dessert that doesn't taste overly sweet, which is a nice change of pace.

—Linda Leuer, Hamel, MN

- -

PREP: 15 min. • **BAKE:** 30 min. + cooling
MAKES: 12 pieces

- ½   cup butter, softened
- 1   cup honey
- 2   large eggs, room temperature
- ½   cup plain yogurt
- 1   tsp. vanilla extract
- 2   cups all-purpose flour
- 2   tsp. baking powder
- ½   tsp. salt
     Assorted fresh fruit and additional honey
     Chopped pistachios, optional

1. Preheat the oven to 350°. Grease a 9-in. cast-iron skillet.
2. In a large bowl, beat butter and honey until blended. Add eggs, 1 at a time, beating well after each addition. Beat in yogurt and vanilla. In another bowl, whisk flour, baking powder and salt; add to butter mixture. Transfer batter to prepared skillet.
3. Bake until a toothpick inserted in center of cake comes out clean, 30-35 minutes. Cool cake completely in pan on a wire rack. Serve with fruit, additional honey and, if desired, chopped pistachios.
Freeze option: Securely wrap cooled cake in foil; freeze. To use, thaw at room temperature and top as directed.
1 piece: 248 cal., 9g fat (5g sat. fat), 53mg chol., 257mg sod., 40g carb. (24g sugars, 1g fiber), 4g pro.

❄ LEMON BLUEBERRY WHOOPIE PIES

These whoopie pies are soft, cakey cookies studded with tart, juicy blueberries and filled with tangy cream cheese frosting. I bring them to family and school events and they are always the first thing gone! Make sure to continually scrape the sides of the bowl with a spatula while making the batter and frosting.
—*Kathy Martino, Pittsburgh, PA*

- -

PREP: 30 min. • **BAKE:** 10 min./batch + cooling
MAKES: 1 dozen

- ½ cup butter, softened
- ½ cup sugar
- 1 large egg, room temperature
- 1 tsp. vanilla extract
- 1¼ cups plus 1 Tbsp. all-purpose flour, divided
- ½ tsp. baking powder
- ¼ tsp. baking soda
- ¼ tsp. salt
- ¼ cup buttermilk
- 1 cup fresh or frozen blueberries
- 2 tsp. grated lemon zest

FILLING

- ¼ cup butter, softened
- ¼ cup cream cheese, softened
- 1 Tbsp. honey
- 1 tsp. grated lemon zest
- ½ tsp. vanilla extract
- 1½ cups confectioners' sugar

1. Preheat oven to 350°. Line baking sheets with silicone baking mats or parchment.
2. In a large bowl, cream butter and sugar until light and fluffy, 5-7 minutes. Beat in egg and vanilla. In another bowl, whisk 1¼ cups flour, baking powder, baking soda and salt; add to creamed mixture alternately with buttermilk, beating well after each addition. In another bowl, toss blueberries and lemon zest with remaining 1 Tbsp. flour; gently fold into dough.
3. Drop dough by tablespoonfuls 2 in. apart onto prepared baking sheets. Bake until edges just begin to brown, 10-12 minutes. Cool on baking sheets 2 minutes. Remove to wire racks to cool completely.
4. For filling, in a large bowl, beat butter and cream cheese until blended. Beat in honey, lemon zest and vanilla. Gradually beat in confectioners' sugar until smooth. Spread on bottoms of half the cookies; cover with remaining cookies. Refrigerate cookies in an airtight container.
Freeze option: Freeze whoopie pies in freezer containers in a single layer (do not stack). To use, thaw before serving.
Note: If using frozen blueberries, use without thawing to avoid discoloring the batter.
1 whoopie pie: 281 cal., 14g fat (8g sat. fat), 51mg chol., 218mg sod., 38g carb. (26g sugars, 1g fiber), 3g pro.

❄ MINT-CHOCOLATE BOMBE

This is a refreshing dessert you can keep in the freezer and take out anytime.
—*Mary Kisinger, Medicine Hat, AB*

- -

PREP: 15 min. + freezing • **MAKES:** 12 servings

- 1 cup heavy whipping cream
- ⅓ cup sweetened condensed milk
- 3 Tbsp. green creme de menthe
- 2 cups chocolate ice cream, softened if necessary
- 3 cups vanilla ice cream, softened if necessary
- 20 chocolate wafers, coarsely crushed
  Optional: Chocolate syrup and chopped Andes mint candies

1. Line a 1½-qt. bowl with plastic wrap. Place in freezer 30 minutes. In a large bowl, beat cream until it begins to thicken. Add milk and creme de menthe; beat until soft peaks form. Quickly spread onto bottom and up sides of bowl to within ½ in. of top. Freeze 2 hours or until firm. Spread chocolate ice cream over mint layer. Freeze 1 hour or until firm.
2. Spoon vanilla ice cream into ice cream shell, spreading to completely cover the top of the shell. Cover and freeze overnight.
3. Invert bombe onto a serving plate. Remove bowl and plastic wrap. Top with wafers. Cut into wedges. If desired, top with chocolate syrup and chopped candies.
1 piece: 270 cal., 15g fat (9g sat. fat), 48mg chol., 118mg sod., 28g carb. (23g sugars, 1g fiber), 4g pro.

LEMON BLUEBERRY WHOOPIE PIES

FROZEN KEY LIME DELIGHT

OLD-TIME CAKE DOUGHNUTS

❄
FROZEN KEY LIME DELIGHT

In the middle of summer, nothing hits the spot quite like this sublime Key lime dessert. Cold, creamy and tart, it looks like sunshine.
—Melissa Millwood, Lyman, SC

- -

PREP: 1 hour + freezing • **MAKES:** 8 servings

1	cup all-purpose flour
½	cup salted cashews, chopped
½	cup sweetened shredded coconut
¼	cup packed light brown sugar
½	cup butter, melted
2	cups heavy whipping cream
1½	cups sweetened condensed milk
1	cup Key lime juice
3	tsp. grated Key lime zest
1	tsp. vanilla extract
	Optional: Whipped cream and Key lime slices

1. Preheat oven to 350°. In a small bowl, combine flour, cashews, coconut and brown sugar. Stir in butter. Sprinkle into a greased 15x10x1-in. baking pan. Bake 20-25 minutes or until golden brown, stirring once. Cool on a wire rack.

2. Meanwhile, in a large bowl, combine cream, milk, lime juice, zest and vanilla. Refrigerate until chilled.

3. Pour the chilled mixture into an ice cream maker, filling the cylinder two-thirds full; freeze according to the manufacturer's directions.

4. Sprinkle half the cashew mixture into an ungreased 11x7-in. pan. Spread ice cream over top; sprinkle with remaining cashew mixture. Cover and freeze 4 hours or until firm. Garnish individual servings with whipped cream and lime slices if desired.

1 piece: 672 cal., 46g fat (27g sat. fat), 131mg chol., 258mg sod., 60g carb. (42g sugars, 1g fiber), 9g pro.

❄ OLD-TIME CAKE DOUGHNUTS

This tender cake doughnut is a piece of heaven at breakfast. For a variation, try adding a dash of rum extract or 1 tablespoon of dark rum.
—*Alissa Stehr, Gau-Odernheim, Germany*

- -

PREP: 30 min. + chilling • **COOK:** 5 min./batch
MAKES: about 2 dozen

2 Tbsp. unsalted butter, softened
1½ cups sugar, divided
3 large eggs, room temperature
4 cups all-purpose flour
1 Tbsp. baking powder
3 tsp. ground cinnamon, divided
½ tsp. salt
⅛ tsp. ground nutmeg
¾ cup 2% milk
Oil for deep-fat frying

1. In a large bowl, beat butter and 1 cup sugar until crumbly, about 2 minutes. Add eggs, 1 at a time, beating well after each addition.
2. Combine the flour, baking powder, 1 tsp. cinnamon, salt and nutmeg; add to butter mixture alternately with milk, beating well after each addition. Cover and refrigerate 2 hours.
3. Turn onto a heavily floured surface; pat dough to ¼-in. thickness. Cut with a floured 2½-in. doughnut cutter. In an electric skillet or deep fryer, heat oil to 375°.
4. Fry doughnuts, a few at a time, until golden brown on both sides. Drain on paper towels.
5. Combine remaining ½ cup sugar and 2 tsp. cinnamon; roll warm doughnuts in mixture.
Freeze option: After frying, wrap doughnuts in foil and transfer to a resealable freezer container. May be frozen for up to 3 months. To use, remove foil and thaw doughnuts at room temperature. Warm if desired. Combine ½ cup sugar and 2 tsp. cinnamon; roll warm doughnuts in mixture.
1 doughnut: 198 cal., 8g fat (1g sat. fat), 30mg chol., 112mg sod., 29g carb. (13g sugars, 1g fiber), 3g pro.

Index